THE LIVING CHRIST

THE LIVING CHRIST

'IN CHRIST' THROUGH SCRIPTURE AND LITURGY

*

J. D. CRICHTON

COLLINS

Collins Liturgical Publications
8 Grafton Street, London W1X 3LA

Collins Liturgical in USA
Icehouse One — 401
151 Union Street, San Francisco, CA 94111-1299

Collins Liturgical in Canada
Novalis, Box 9700, Terminal,
375 Rideau St, Ottawa, Ontario K1G 4B4

Distributed in Ireland by
Educational Company of Ireland
21 Talbot Street, Dublin 1

Collins Liturgical Australia
PO Box 316, Blackburn, Victoria 3130

Collins Liturgical New Zealand
PO Box 1, Auckland

ISBN 0 00 599090 4

First published 1988

Library of Congress Cataloging-in-Publication Data

Crichton, J. D. (James Dunlop), — —
Living in Christ

1. Christian life—Catholic authors. 2. Jesus Christ—Biography.
3. Christian biography—Palestine
I. Title
BX2350.2.C68 1988 232.9'01 87-31984
ISBN 0-00-599090-4

Cover photo is a reproduction of a handpainted icon from
Pisca Design, Woodford Green, Essex

Typographical design Colin Reed
Typeset by Burgess & Son (Abingdon) Ltd
Printed in Great Britain by

CONTENTS

Acknowledgements

Scripture quotations (except for the psalms) are taken from the Revised Standard Version apart from one or two from the Jerusalem Bible.

The psalms are quoted from *The Psalms: a New Translation.* © The Grail (England) 1963, published by Collins.

Some phrases from the Prayer of the Church are taken from *The Divine Office,* The Liturgy of the Hours (Collins, Dwyer, Talbot, 1974).

PREFACE

In this small book I have tried to express certain ponderings of many years on the meaning of being 'in Christ', an expression that I understand is used by St Paul more than a hundred and fifty times. 'Being in Christ' evidently means living in Christ, being open to the action of Christ within us and responding to him with faith and love and by the way we live. It is what St Paul meant by the phrase the 'imitation of Christ' which has often been interpreted in an externalist way; we must try and act as Christ would have acted in this or that circumstance. Apart from the fact that he was unique, he also lived at a different time from us, in a different country and in a different culture and there may well be occasions when we can't say how he would have acted. Rather, St Paul can say 'Have this mind among yourselves, which also was in Jesus Christ' (Philippians 2.5), and then he goes on to show us the consequences: self-humiliation and obedience to God manifested in the birth, passion, death and resurrection of Christ. But such 'imitation' is first interior and, according to temperaments and circumstances, will have very various manifestations. Men like St Athanasius and St Cyprian could write of the necessity to flee from persecutors or enemies as martyrdom was not right for them at that time or perhaps at all. Cyprian died for Christ. Athanasius did not.

But there was an 'imitation', the most striking and radical, martyrdom itself, and until about the year 400 the martyr was the 'saint' *tout court* because his dying for Christ was the total and complete imitation of Christ. By his dying he shared in the death of Christ and was immediately exalted to share in the life of the Risen Lord. Later, saints showed that by living *for* Christ they could imitate him but they would say that their living for Christ was only possible because they were 'in Christ' and Christ was living in them.

But this was not, and is not, special to the saints. It was the burden of so much that St Paul and St John said to the first Christians, like the wayward Galatians to whom Paul could write 'You are all sons of God ... you have put on Christ ... you are all one in Christ Jesus' so that like Paul they could say 'It is no longer I who live, but Christ lives in me' (Galatians 3.26,28; 2.20). Pondering on this and similar texts and writing (probably) on the eucharist, a Greek writer of the fourteenth century, Nicholas Cabasilas, could say of Christ: 'He is the Host whose presence fills our whole being ... It is he whom we receive and not just something from him ... He compenetrates us so as to form one spirit with us; for at once our body, our soul, our faculties become spiritual. There is a union of soul with soul, body with body, blood with blood'.[1] So vivid a realization of union with Christ may be disconcerting for some but it is to say no more than the often repeated saying of Jesus 'I will be in you and you will be in me'. It just unfolds what that saying means.

But the very title of Cabasilas' book, *Life in Christ,* is significant. It is not a life *of* Christ showing how we can 'imitate' him. It is about life in Christ which we are all called to live. For me it was a section of part III of St

[1] French trans. *La Vie–Jésus-Christ* (1960), p. 100.

Thomas' *Summa Theologica, De Vita Christi,* which sums up so much of the patristic tradition, that years ago prompted me to look into the matter further. It showed me that certain great events of Christ's life, his baptism, his temptation, his transfiguration, his prayer and the rest were not just events that concerned him but that in them is a vital force that comes to us through the Church, through the liturgy, and through our private prayer. As St Leo said, the events were not just 'examples' but sources of life that are still available to us. When they are celebrated as liturgical feasts that life is being communicated to us if we will approach Christ with open hearts in faith and love. That is what this book is about. We can go beyond just thinking about these past events, we can go beyond merely commemorating them or meditating on them. We can make a living contact with the living Christ who is just as 'real', just as near to us, as he was when he was with his disciples and spoke to them.

THE BIRTH

*

CHRISTMAS, as everyone knows, has its own special atmosphere. There is the good will and the kindliness, the giving of presents, the gathering of families, the concern for the lonely and those in want, and that special spirit that can hardly be defined. For Christians there is the midnight eucharist, the carols and the crib. But what is Christmas really all about?

Too often our understanding of it goes no deeper than a consideration of the gospel passages that are read out at the Christmas Masses. The birth of Jesus is something that happened long ago. We are grateful for it, we thank God for 'the goodness and loving kindness' (*philanthropia*) that appeared in our Saviour. But all this remains external to us. It is good of course to meditate on God's love and goodness to us as shown in his Son, Jesus, but that is rather our movement towards him than a realization that the coming of the Son in the flesh is God's movement towards us. It is necessary to say that that movement continues into the present. God offers us his saving love *now* and comes to us in a new way every time we celebrate the Christmas feast.

How can that be? God approaches us first in his

word. We hear the gospel proclaimed to us: 'I bring you news of great joy, *Evangelizo vobis gaudium magnum*', I proclaim the Good News to you: a Saviour is born to us. *That* is the Good News and it is of today as much as it was of yesterday. Christ is present in his word, it is he himself who speaks when the holy scriptures are read in church, he is still proclaiming his gospel (Constitution on the Liturgy, 7, 33). Through the proclamation of the gospel at Midnight Mass Christ is approaching us, offering himself to us as really as he did when he spoke to the people two thousand years ago. But as then so now, he looks to us for a response and it is in that response that he makes himself present to us. He is with us, he is Immanuel.

> We may not be able to penetrate to the full meaning of the mystery of God becoming one of us but we have the words of the gospels and the prophets to instruct us and kindle our faith. It is thus that we can perceive the birth of the Lord *as present* and not simply as a past event which we recall. The proclamation of the angel of the Lord to the shepherds keeping watch over their flocks has filled our ears also . . . it is as if on this feast it was said once more 'Behold, I bring you good news of great joy which will come to all the people; for to you today is born this day in the city of David a Saviour who is Christ the Lord' (Leo, *De Nativitate*, IX).

We have the word of the prophet and we hear Isaiah announce the coming of the Messiah:

> A child is born for us, a son is given to us and this is the name they give him:

Wonderful Counsellor, Mighty God,
Eternal Father, Prince of Peace.

We have the words of the Apostle that at first sight seem to be no more than an exhortation to holy living but he begins by speaking of the 'appearing' of God's grace which has made salvation possible. Jesus is the 'epiphany' of God's redeeming love, he is the incarnation of God's movement towards us, and that there might be a life-giving encounter between ourselves and God he sacrificed himself to set us free from all wickedness and to purify us so that we could become his own people. All this began when the Son of God became a man 'for when we celebrate the coming in flesh of our Saviour we are celebrating the origin of the Christian people. Head and members have but one birthday and at Christmas we are born again' through the birth of Christ (Leo, *De Nativitate*, VI).

At the Dawn Mass we hear the Apostle again as he proclaims not only that the Saviour has been revealed but that he comes to us with his love through the water of rebirth, which the pagans cried out for and vainly sought, and he makes us new, inserting into us the Holy Spirit so that our relationship with God may be established and we can become heirs with Jesus, the only Son of the Father. Christmas is the celebration of the renewal of our rebirth in Christ and year by year we are made new first by faith, a faith that is aroused by the proclamation of the word in which Christ is present, and then by sacrament. The word is creative of Christ's life within us if we will but open our minds and hearts to him. By the word we are called again, as mankind has been throughout the course of history. But there is something more:

> The whole assembly of the people who have come forth from the baptismal font and have been crucified with Christ in his passion, raised to life in his resurrection and set at the right hand of God in his ascension, are born (*congeniti*) with him in his birth which we celebrate today (Leo, *De Nativitate*, VI).

Baptism in which the new life is generated is the link between ourselves and the incarnation and the redemption. It is only in later centuries that they became separated—at least in thought. The birth was the beginning of Jesus' redeeming work and his whole life carried that work forward until it reached its climax in the suffering of the cross and the glory of the resurrection: 'According to God's plan of salvation the sin of the world must be destroyed by the *birth* and passion of Jesus Christ, and its effects flow to every succeeding generation' (Leo, *De Nativitate*, III). As we say in the Office of Christmas Eve: 'Tomorrow the sin of the world will be destroyed' and 'Lift up your heads, your redemption is at hand.'

Redemption is made our own by union with God through Jesus Christ. We are called to be and are the adopted sons and daughters of God, and so it is that we read on the Second Sunday after Christ: 'Blessed be the God and Father of our Lord Jesus Christ who has blessed us with all spiritual blessings of heaven *in Christ.* Before the world was made, he chose us, *chose us in Christ*, to be holy and spotless, and *to live* through Jesus in his presence, determining that we should become *his adopted sons* through Jesus Christ ... to the praise of his glorious grace ... which he freely bestowed on us *in the Beloved*' (Ephesians 1.3–6). Through the Son's taking of our human nature, through the very Sonship of Christ, we are made sons and daughters of God: 'The Word was made flesh and to all who received him, who believed in his name, he gave power to become children of God' (John 1.14,12). Through the 'enfleshed' Word we enter into the family of God, into the life of the Holy Trinity which is a life of a totally self-giving love and supreme energy. Shaped and formed after the fashion of the Son and through the Holy Spirit whom he gives to us we have access to the Father and even now are able to share the life and love that is God. This is the inner reality that the Church prays for at Christmas. We praise God for the wonder of the creation of the human race and for its even more wonderful redemption and we ask that as his Son took to himself our human nature we might be made sharers in his divine nature (Collect, Third Mass). Immediately we are reminded of the phase in 2 Peter 1.4 where we are told that thanks to the gracious promises of God 'we become partakers of the divine nature'. The divine energy is at work in us, enlightening our minds and kindling our love so that we may have a real relationship with God in the depths of our being. This relationship is such that we can be said to bear the 'form' or character of the Son, in our nature that he took upon himself. This is what the Christmas liturgy calls the 'sacred exchange'. The Son of God has become man and we are drawn into the life of God by the very flesh that is now next to the Father in heaven.

Nor is the adoption simply a once-for-all event, given in baptism. By our celebration of the Christmas festival our filial relationship with God is renewed and strengthened. We are moving on the way to the consummation of which St John wrote:

> We are God's children now; yet it does not appear what we shall be, but we know that when he appears we shall be like him, for we shall see him as he is (1 John 3.2).

This then is the reality that underlies the simple story of Christmas, this is what is important amidst the carols, the present-giving and all the more or less secular jollity of the season. If Christmas is the feast of the child it is because the Child of God made and makes it possible for us to be his children, and if it is a feast of the family it is first the feast of the family of God 'from whom all fatherhood in heaven and on earth is named'. But it is also the feast of the people of God who are members of the Body that is the Church, bound together by the gifts of God, faith and love and life.

All this is what is given or at least offered and it is

this that we must translate into the conduct of our daily life:

> Let us give thanks to the Father through his Son in the Holy Spirit who out of the great mercy with which he loved us, took pity on us even when we were dead on account of our sins so that in him we might be a new creature, reshaped by his hand. Let us then strip off our old self with its behaviour and since we have been made sharers in the birth (*generationis*) of Christ let us renounce the deeds of the flesh. Christian, I beg you, be aware of your dignity and since you have been made a sharer in the divine nature do not return to your former baseness by an unworthy life. Call to mind the Head, think of the Body of which you are a member and do not forget that you have been snatched from the power of darkness and have been carried over into God's light, God's kingdom. By the sacrament of baptism you have been made a temple of the Holy Spirit. Do not by wicked deeds (depraved conduct) make yourself once again the slave of the devil. For you were bought at the price of the blood of Christ and he who has redeemed you will one day judge you in truth (Leo, *De Nativitate*, I).

We have the word of God in the scriptures and at Christmas this inevitably reminds us of the Word that was made flesh and our nature that he has made his own and would give us: 'I am the bread of life ... if anyone eats this bread he will live for ever and the bread which I shall give for the life of the world is my flesh' (John 6.51). And the bread of life that he promised he gives us: 'Take, this is my body ... This is my blood of the covenant which is poured out for many' (Mark 14.23,24). He gives himself to us so that he can be in us and we can be in him; flesh, though veiled, meets flesh and we become one body, one Spirit with him. Every Christmas is a communion with the incarnate Lord.

By word, by baptism, by the eucharist we are renewed, born again, for it is Jesus 'who receives us into himself and we receive him into ourselves. The Lord Jesus in his birth became our flesh and we become his by our rebirth. We are members of his body and temples of the Holy Spirit' (Leo, *De Nativitate*, III).

THE SHOWING

*

ALTHOUGH the Christmas feast is bathed in light it is mostly concerned with the Birth. The Epiphany, the Manifestation, the Showing, is largely concerned with light:

> Arise, shine out, for your light has come,
> the glory of the Lord is rising on you
> though the night still covers the earth
> and darkness the peoples (Isaiah 60.1-2).

We hear these words first in the Office of Readings and then at Mass. The theme comes again and again throughout the Office:

> The Lord is king, let earth rejoice ...
> Light shines forth for the just
> and joy for the upright of heart.
> Rejoice, you just, in the Lord;
> give glory to his holy name (Psalm 96(97)).

> He is a light in darkness for the upright:
> he is generous, merciful, and just (Psalm 111(112)).

The light is revelation, the relevation of Jesus, King and Lord, the Son of God who now in the fullness of time shows the glory of God by this, the greatest of his saving acts, his appearance on earth as the Saviour of the world. He is the manifestation of the Father who dwells in light inaccesible. He is the Word who was with God and now becomes flesh and dwells among us, full of grace and truth, so that all can see his glory, 'glory as of the only Son of God' (John 1.14). He would share that glory with us and does so with everyone who will believe in him. It is he who enlightens every man coming into this world, it is through him that a ray of the divine light penetrates the minds and hearts of human beings so that they become children of light, in their turn reflecting the light to others.

It is the revelation of the Son of God-made-man that prompts our praise and our thanksgiving:

> Let the heavens rejoice and earth be glad,
> let the sea and all within it thunder praise,
> let the land and all it bears rejoice,
> all the trees of the wood shout for joy
> at the presence of the Lord for he comes,
> he comes to rule the earth ... (Psalm 95(96)).

But if we are to break out in praise and thanksgiving we must first contemplate the wonder of God coming close to man. The light of the star led the magi to the crib and they represented the 'peoples of the world' and were the first of the Gentiles to accept the Saviour in faith. Faith is indeed an enlightening but through the years it must grow until in the end we can contemplate the beauty of God face to face (collect of the day).

Faith is the light as yet occluded by our inadequacies, by our passions, by our self-centredness but also because the splendour of God must be veiled by the cloud of unknowing, for 'no man can see God and live'. Yet we can come to God through Jesus for when we 'see' him by the eyes of faith we see the Father (John 14.9). In her 'showings', when Julian of Norwich 'saw' the Father and the whole of creation like a hazel nut in his hand, she saw him through the veil of the suffering Christ who had become most vivid to her imagination. Perhaps the direction is different for us. As we contemplate Jesus in his birth, in his manifestations, in his baptism, in the events of his ministry and in the climactic accomplishment of his saving work in suffering, death and resurrection, we catch glimpses of the glory of God. The glory of God shone on the shepherds, 'we have beheld his glory' said St John, the glory revealed in his birth, the glory of the Father that is reflected in the Son who bears the very stamp of his nature (Hebrews 1.3). How are we to think of this glory? There was little that was glorious in the stable of Bethlehem, nothing that was glorious in the passion and the death. But these events and all the others of Jesus' ministry were symbols, what St John calls signs of the creative love of God made present and effective in the saving work of his Son. For John, the whole of Christ's life was a revealing of the 'glory' of God and for him the light of the resurrection casts its ray back onto the birth, the life, the suffering and the death. The glory was revealed in the raising of Lazarus (11.40); it was to be revealed again in Jesus' death: 'Father save me from this hour? No, for this purpose I have come to this hour. Father glorify thy name. Then a voice came from heaven, "I have glorified it and I will glorify it again"' (John 12.27). When the hour had in fact come he prayed 'Father ... glorify thy Son that the Son may glorify thee ... I glorified thee on earth, having accomplished the work which thou gavest me to do; and now, Father, glorify thou me in thy own presence with the glory which I had with thee before the world was made' (John 17. 1–5).

The whole of the gospel of St John can be seen as an epiphany of the Lord Christ. There are the seven 'signs' or miracles that draw people to him, there is the glory that is to be discerned through his life and deeds, and there is the light which he himself says that he is: 'I am the light of the world; he who follows me will not walk in darkness but will have the light of life.' The interpretation of this saying is not obvious and the experts tell us that Christ is light as the giver of the new revelation—himself and his teaching. If we approach him in faith we are 'enlightened' as were the catechumens by baptism. We no longer belong to the 'darkness' which is the world exiled from God, perhaps self-exiled, the world where the regenerative power of Christ has not penetrated or where it has been refused. Even so, faith is not just a believing with the mind, an assent to a truth, even a revealed truth. A writer of the Johannine school shows that faith is a vital moving of the whole person to Jesus, the Son of God: 'Everyone who believes that Jesus is the Christ is a child of God and everyone who loves the parent loves the child ... whatever is born of God overcomes the world; and this is the victory that overcomes the world, our faith', (1 John 5.1,5) that is, faith in Jesus who is the Son of God. Faith is dynamic; it moves us to adherence to Christ, to union with him. It is the first entering into the life of Christ. It is not just a (partial) illumination of the intellect. It is like the sun that assists at the birth of life, that in fact is indispensable to its coming into existence. Jesus himself is the light, he dwells within us and we become children of light so that we can become 'the light of the world', like John the Baptist bearing witness to the light that enlightens everyone who will receive him in faith.

Christ is the light, the Word and splendour of the Father. He is 'the light of the nations', making known the Father and his unfailing love for them. He is the light within us. In setting up his tent among us (John 1.14) he became the 'place' where the glory of God dwells; he is the Shekinah of old, the brooding presence of Yahweh over the tabernacle, now brought to perfection in the dwelling of the Word among us. He is the true Temple and his body is the Church (John 2.19–21). But each one of us is a temple of the Lord through our union with the incarnate Son and by the operation of the Holy Spirit who is given to us. And as the whole Church is illuminated by the light of Christ so that it can proclaim his truth (John 15.13), so is each one of us. By the light that is in us we respond to the light and thus we can lay hold of the truth that is revealed in Jesus Christ who is Truth itself.

Like the incarnation the Epiphany is but the beginning of a process. Its dynamism continues to this day when, in faith, we contemplate the Word made flesh and receive him into ourselves. This was the theme of two ancient liturgical prayers in the Gelasian Sacramentary:[1]

> Shed your light upon your people, Lord, and illuminate our hearts that we may come to the eternal splendour of our home in heaven.
>
> The presence of the light in us now is the pledge that one day we shall see God face to face and seeing him become like him.

Another prayer asks that the light that began to shine on the magi may grow to its fullness in us:

> Lord God, by the mystery of this festival you have shed on all nations a light that is eternal; grant your people the knowledge of the splendour of their Redeemer. *May*

[1] The prayers quoted below are to be found in: J. Lemarié, *La Manifestation du Seigneur. La Liturgie de Noël et de l'Épiphanie* (Paris, 1957), pp. 274–5.

that light grow ever clearer within them so that they may come to the light that never fails.

Another prayer from the Bergamo Sacramentary underlines that the light is within us and that it is destined to grow through the celebration of the liturgical feast:

> Lord God, you have dedicated this day by the election of the Gentiles, the first-fruits of your redeeming work, and through the spendour of the star you have manifested yourself to us; grant that this new light may rise in our hearts like the sun in all its brilliance.

That phrase 'the first-fruits of your redeeming work' suggests another line of thought. The Epiphany is not just a historical commemoration. It is a celebration of the mystery of Christ that was revealed long ago, the mystery that was not simply a person but an action, the redeeming work of passion, death and resurrection and it is of this that the 'Gentiles', that is ourselves, are the 'first-fruits'. That is why the canticle of the First Vespers of the feast is the passage from 1 Timothy 3.16: 'Great indeed is the mystery of our religion' said the writer:

> He was manifested in the flesh,
> vindicated in the Spirit,
> seen by angels,
> preached among the nations,
> believed in by the world,
> taken up in glory.

Here is the whole mystery of Christ from the Epiphany to his ascension in glory. He is active in the Church on which came the Holy Spirit who 'proved' that Jesus was in the right so that the nations could believe in him and see, in his ascent to the glory of the Father, the divine endorsement of his saving work. The Christ who 'was manifested in the flesh', the Christ whose light shone on the peoples of his time, is still with us in word and sacrament, above all in the eucharist where we are invited to respond to the light that shines eternally. As it were impersonating the magi who offered gold, frankincense and myrrh, we come before God with our gifts, the symbols of our self-offering which become sacrament, the very reality that is Jesus Christ:

> Lord, look with favour on your Church's gifts: no longer gold, frankincense and myrrh, but he of whom those offerings were but symbols, Jesus Christ your Son, our Lord, offered by us and received back as our food' (Prayer over the Gifts, trans. *The Layman's Missal*, 1963).

If there were any doubt about this element of the Epiphany feast it is dispelled by the antiphon to the Benedictus of Lauds, an ancient Greek text that is usually passed over with too little notice:

> Today the Church is united to the heavenly Bridegroom, for in the Jordan Christ has washed away her sins; to the royal nuptials the magi come in haste with their gifts and at the wedding feast water is changed into wine to the joy of the guests.

Clearly this text is about Christ's saving work, the effect of which is considered to be present: the Church *is* united to the Bridegroom and now experiences the joy of the wedding feast. The antiphon sees the saving work as beginning in the coming of Christ in the flesh and consequently here is to be found the origin of the Christian people. But it will be convenient to consider this text at greater length in the context of the Baptism of Christ.

This is sufficient to show that the feast is not just a commemoration of the past, and the Epiphany itself was not just the showing forth of Jesus as the Son of God. As so many of the liturgical texts indicate, Jesus is revealed as King and Lord; as the Lord who by his loving obedience and his self-humiliation in the passion, death and resurrection was the Saviour of the human race. It was for this reason that the Father exalted him and for this reason that every tongue must confess that Jesus Christ is Lord, the Lord of all that is in heaven or on earth (Philippians 2.7–11). And even in his incarnation, even in his manifestation, as also in his baptism and at the marriage feast, he was active and his saving action is communicated to us in the celebration of the liturgical feast. Our vision then turns not so much to the past as to the present. Christ, the light of life, is still bringing life, still enlightening our minds and still inserting his saving energy into our lives.

That is why St Leo could write:

> This day is not so much a thing of the past that the power of what was once revealed is now ineffectual. It is not only a memory preserved by faith or recalled in honour. God's gift is renewed and we in our time experience what happened in the beginning (*De Epiphania*, VI).

From this perspective we can the better appreciate the emphasis on vocation and mission that is so prominent in the Western liturgy. Unworthy as we are we have received a gift, we have received the light so that it can shine out from ourselves and by word and example we can bear witness to the eternal Christ.

This is our vocation, the fruit of Christ's redeeming work, but it makes certain demands of us:

> Instructed by the mysteries of divine grace, let us celebrate with spiritual joy the day of our birth (*primitiarum nostrarum*) and the beginning of the calling of the Gentiles. Let us give thanks to the God of mercy who 'has qualified us to share in the inheritance of the saints in light, who has delivered us from the domination of darkness and transferred us to the kingdom of his beloved Son ...' Let us to the best of our ability bend our will to the grace which calls all to Christ. For whoever lives a godly and chaste life, whoever seeks those things that are above and not those things on earth, is like that heavenly light, and he who preserves the brightness of a holy life is like a star showing to others the way that leads to God. You should all have a care to be helpful to one another and then in the kingdom of God you will shine like children of the light (*De Epiphania*, III).

Christ is the Light, Christ is the light of life and that life, ultimately Christ himself, is renewed within us by the word and sacrament we celebrate on the Feast of the Epiphany.

THE BAPTISM

*

THE baptism of Christ is liturgically more closely connected to the Epiphany than is usually thought. We have already considered the antiphon of the Benedictus (page 16) and it seems appropriate to associate with it another for the Magnificat of Second Vespers:

> We celebrate the holy day marked by three miracles:
> today magi were led by the star to the crib;
> at the wedding feast the water was changed into wine;
> today Christ willed to be baptized in the Jordan to bring us salvation.

These two texts may seem to be out of place if the Epiphany is regarded, as it has been in the West since the time of St Augustine, as a missionary feast. In fact they are an indication that there is an older stratum in the celebration and a reminder that it came from the East, where it has always been associated with water. The remote origins of the feast are to be found in Egypt as a pagan celebration of the rising of the Nile, indispensable for the whole agricultural economy of the country. The various stages of the feast's development need not be traced here. All we need say is that early in the Byzantine tradition, baptism formed the main theme of the feast and now it is simply a feast of baptism which in a later development has led to the rite of the blessing of the sea.[1] In the West, apart from these two texts, the theme of baptism has been allowed to fall out—though the placing of the feast of the Baptism of the Lord on the Sunday after Epiphany has done something to restore its importance to the Western liturgy.

There are two ways of looking at it. The baptism of Christ and the wedding feast at Cana are manifestations, epiphanies, of the power of the Lord. The baptism spells out the declaration of the Father that Jesus is indeed the promised Messiah and that he is no earthly king but his Son, the Beloved, the Chosen One, on whom the Father's favour rests. As St John shows, the wedding feast was the 'first of the signs' which 'manifested his glory' with the consequence that 'his disciples believed in him'. This brings it into line with the manifestation to the magi who fell on their knees and worshipped him.

But there is another way of seeing these two events as they are celebrated in the liturgy. As an approach to an understanding of the baptism one can ask: Was it an event that, apart from the divine attestation,

[1] In the Byzantine rite the water for baptism is blessed on the Vigil of Epiphany. This blessing sometimes takes place outside, by a river or by the sea (See Timothy Ware, *The Orthodox Church* (1963) p. 307). Its sense is that the whole element of water is blessed.

concerned Jesus alone? Did what happened then have certain consequences? In earlier ages the Church had a profound conviction that there was something here that is of importance to all Christians. It was not a single cut-off event; it was a redemptive act of God in Christ. It was the inauguration of a whole process that will continue to the end of time. Christ's baptism was *for* us.

Let us then consider the Benedictus antiphon in the context of the Baptism:

> Today the Church is united to the heavenly Bridegroom, for in the Jordan Christ has washed away her sins; to the royal nuptials the magi come in haste with their gifts, and at the wedding feast water is changed into wine to the joy of the guests.

The first thing that may strike the modern Western Christian as unusual if not odd is the relating of the bridal theme with the Baptism. We are inclined to protest: how could the Church which did not yet exist have its sins washed away and be united with the heavenly Bridegroom? And how can the event of the coming of the magi have anything to do with the bridal theme of the Baptism? And what has the changing of the water into wine to do with the marriage of the Church? One theme that binds them together is that of 'manifestation'. All these events were, as we have seen, manifestations of what St John calls the glory of God revealed in Christ and in all the 'works' that Christ did. But that does not exhaust the meaning of either this antiphon or that of the Magnificat. As we have seen, we have here an Eastern understanding of the feast and this takes us into a realm that is foreign to the modern mind.

Often the liturgy is not concerned with chronology, and the ancient seasons and feasts are not mere historical commemorations of past events. They are celebrations of the mystery of Christ in its various phases which were gradually spaced out in time but which are all aspects of the one mystery that is Christ (Colossians 1.37). But the Christian mystery has its roots in the past and reaches on into the future at the same time as having a present reality. The early Christian writers, especially those who wrote in Greek and Syriac, saw the Church as containing within itself the 'church' of the Old Testament as well as that of the New Testament. This is a view that goes back to the Book of the Apocalypse. The Woman who brings forth the male child is a symbol of the *two* churches: the people of Israel who according to the plan of God were destined for salvation, and the new Israel in which that salvation was being realized. In the union of human nature with the Son of God there was to be seen the beginning of the new marriage covenant between God and the human race. Very early on Christians saw in the womb of Mary the bridal bed, the *thalamus*, in which the new people of God received their existence (cf Psalm 18(19).6).

If we would understand this we must realize that

these early writers were not thinking of the institutional church, the visible society as it appears and exists in the world of affairs. They were thinking of the Body, indwelt by Christ and the Holy Spirit, which indeed exists in time but transcends it. In Christ himself, the Messiah, the whole of the old church is represented and in a sense concretized, and it is Christ who through the mystery of salvation makes it the new people of God:

> You were at one time separated from Christ, alienated from the commonwealth of Israel, and strangers to the covenant . . . But now in Christ Jesus you who were once far off have been brought near in the blood of Christ. For he is our peace, who has made both one, and broken down the dividing wall of hostility, by abolishing in his flesh the law of commandments and ordinances, that he might create in himself one new man in the place of two, and might reconcile us both to God in one body through the cross, thereby bringing the hostility to an end (Ephesians 2.12–17).

For the liturgy then the Church existed but it needed to be purified from sin, redeemed, and the beginning of that redeeming work is to be found here in the Baptism. Nor is the bridal theme lacking: for this we can go back to the Letter to the Ephesians and beyond it to the Old Testament. There the Church is the bride. She becomes the bride through Christ's love for her and 'by the washing of water with the word', and the writer sees it as being done to the whole Church and as having redemptive significance:

> Christ loved the Church and gave himself up for her, that he might sanctify her, having cleansed her by the washing of water with the word, that he might present the Church to himself in splendour, without spot or wrinkle or any such thing ... (Ephesians 5.25–27).

This marriage-union of Christ with his Church is a 'mystery' of which human marriage is the symbol: 'This mystery is a profound one, and I am saying that it refers to Christ and the Church' (Ephesians 5.32). The relation between the redemption and the Baptism is very close; their meanings seem to run into one another. Perhaps this is not surprising when we recall that Jesus spoke of his death as a baptism which he must undergo (Mark 10.28–40). Thus, as the model of marriage is the union between Christ and his Church, so the model of baptism is the death and resurrection of the Lord.

It may be that in the Letter to the Ephesians, and perhaps in the Benedictus antiphon, there is an obscure reference to an ancient pagan practice, the nuptial bath of the bride. It is not improbable.[2] The world in which the Ephesians lived was familiar with the *hieros gamos*, the sacred wedding, which was the symbol of fertility. But there is another, perhaps even more ancient tradition in the Old Testament which among other places is represented in Isaiah 61.10–11, a passage which was to be found in the former Office of Epiphany:

[2] Cf J. H. Houlden, *Paul's Letters from Prison* (1979), pp. 330–332.

> I will greatly rejoice in the Lord,
> my soul shall exult in my God;
> For he has clothed me with the garments of salvation,
> he has covered me with the robe of righteousness,
> as a bridegroom decks himself with a garland,
> and as a bride adorns herself with jewels.

And as if to suggest that this too is a symbol of fertility, though the fertility will spring forth from God, the passages continues:

> For as the earth brings forth its shoots,
> and as a garden causes what is sown in it to spring up,
> so the Lord God will cause righteousness and praise to spring forth before all nations.

If, with some exegetes, we may see in the changing of the water into wine at least a secondary reference to the eucharist, there is added another dimension of the redeeming mystery. The eucharist is the bridal banquet which makes present the passion, death and resurrection of Christ when we will drink the new wine of the kingdom (Mark 14.25; Luke 22.18; Matthew 26.29).

Through this we are linked with another of the great themes of the Bible, the eschatological banquet. The Day of the Lord, says Isaiah, will be celebrated as a great banquet:

> On this mountain,
> the Lord of hosts will prepare for all people
> a banquet of rich food, a banquet of fine wines,

> of food rich and juicy, of fine strained wines.
> On this mountain he will remove
> the mourning veil covering all peoples,
> and the shroud enwrapping all nations,
> he will destroy death for ever (Isaiah 25.6–7 *JB*).

In the gospels the parable of the marriage feast (Matthew 22.10–14; Luke 14.16–24) is certainly eschatological; and finally (and not to mention other passages) there is in the Apocalypse the marriage feast of the Lamb, the symbol of the achieved union of the Church with God:

> Let us rejoice and exult and give him the glory,
> for the marriage of the Lamb has come,
> and his bride has made herself ready ...
> Blessed are those who are invited to the marriage supper
> of the Lamb' (19.7–9).

And we remember the new Jerusalem, the holy city, 'coming down from God, prepared as a bride adorned for her husband'.

Then the image changes and there is the water that flows through the city, the river of life:

> Then he showed me the river of the water of life, bright as crystal, flowing from the throne of God and the Lamb ... on either side of the river the tree of life ... and the leaves of the tree were for the healing of the nations. There shall no more be anything accursed, but the throne of God and the Lamb shall be in it, and his name shall be on their foreheads. And night shall be no more;

> they need no light or lamp, or sun, for the Lord God will be their light, and they shall reign for ever and ever (Revelation 22.1–5).

Here is a veritable concatenation of Johannine images. There is the Bridegroom and the Bride, there is the light that illuminates the city of God, there is the flowing water that enlivens the whole Church and passes from her to all who would drink it—the nations—to whom it brings healing, redemption. If the Baptism event does not seem to have all these overtones and associations (though we recall that it was the Baptist who in the context of the baptism spoke of Jesus as the 'Lamb who takes away the sin of the world' and who refers to himself as the 'friend of the bridegroom' (John 2.36; 3.39)) the Church, pondering on the event and celebrating it through the centuries, has seen in it great depths of meaning which are thoroughly biblical.

Against this redemptive background we can see that it is not improbable that the Baptism had enduring effects and this was the conviction of the Church both in the East and the West during all the early centuries. To this day we read in the Office part of a sermon of St Gregory Nazianzen on 'The Lights', preached on the feast of the Epiphany in 381 during his short and unhappy reign as Bishop of Constantinople. For him the Baptism was a present reality:

> Again, my Jesus, and again a mystery... a mystery lofty and divine and allied to the Glory above. For the Holy

> Day of the Lights, to which we have come, and which we are celebrating today, has for its origin the Baptism of Christ, the True Light, that enlighteneth every man that cometh into the world, and *effecteth my purification*, and assists that light which we received from the beginning from Him above, but which we darkened and confused by sin.

Christians are in Christ and what he did is done not only for them but in them:

> Christ is illumined, let us shine forth with him. Christ is baptized, let us descend with him that we may also ascend with him.

How this could be is then explained:

> John baptizes. Jesus comes to him ... perhaps to sanctify the Baptist himself, but certainly *to bury the whole of the old Adam in the water;* and before this and for the sake of this, to sanctify Jordan; for as he is Spirit and Flesh, so he consecrates us by the Spirit and water. John will not receive him; Jesus contends: 'I have need to be baptized by Thee', says the Voice to the Word, the Friend to the Bridegroom ....

Gregory continues with a series of antitheses in this vein which are not to our purpose here and then he emphasizes the solidarity of the Christian with Christ who is the New Adam, the head of the body, who as he goes up out of the water

> *with himself carries up the world.* He sees the heaven split open which Adam had shut against himself and all his posterity, as were the gates of Paradise by the flaming

> sword. And the Spirit bears witness to his Godhead, for he descends upon One that is like him, as does the Voice from heaven ... and like a dove seen in bodily form it bestows honour on his body, since this is also God by being deified.[3]

For Gregory, the Baptism is like a pre-enactment of the saving death and resurrection. Jesus goes down into the water taking with him the whole world, the human race. This he indicates in his peroration:

> Wash yourselves and keep yourselves clean. God rejoices in nothing so much as in the amendment and salvation of men on whose behalf is every word and all the sacraments. Be cleansed so that you may be like lights in the world, a life-giving force to all other men, and stand as perfect lights beside that great light, and learn the mystery of the illumination of heaven, enlightened by the Trinity more purely and clearly, *of which even now you are receiving in a measure* the *One Ray* from the one Godhead in Christ Jesus our Lord ...[4]

Baptism was of course called *photismos,* enlightenment, but Gregory is able to combine in one paragraph water, life and light and to suggest the indwelling of the One Ray that beams forth from God.

Other writers have another way to link the Baptism with the Christian in the here and now. For Ambrose

[3] Trans. *Nicene and Post-Nicene Fathers of the Christian Church,* edd. P. Schaff and H. Wace, reprint 1974, VII, p. 357. Last part (because better translation) *The Divine Office* (1974), pp. 379–380.

[4] NPN Fathers, *ibid.*

the water was grace-bearing and, touched by the flesh of Christ, it received the power to baptize. This was a common theme. For John Chrysostom Jesus sanctified the water for those who would be baptized in the future, and Cyril of Jerusalem saw the touch 'of the divine presence' as contributing power to the waters:

> Christ bathed in the river of Jordan and having invested the waters with the divine presence of his body, he emerged from them, and the Holy Spirit visited him in substantial form, like coming on like.[5]

This notion of consecration by contact may not appeal to us now but these writers see the baptism of Jesus as initiating a process that continues in the Church today. Water was sanctified, water was made the apt instrument, as perhaps we would say, for communicating the light and life of Christ to us.

Cyril of Jerusalem in particular sees a very close connection between the baptism of Christ and the baptism of Christians. The former is the model of Christian baptism. The very image of Christ is formed within us so that we become 'icons' of him. Here is the 'imitation of Christ' at its deepest.

> You have been baptized in Christ, you have put on Christ and you have become conformed (*summorphoi*) to

[5] Myst. Cat.3, trans. as in E. Yarnold *The Awe-spiring Rites of Initiation* (1972), p. 79. The references to Ambrose and Chrysostom respectively: *In Luc. Expositio*, lib.2, cap.3; *Op. Imperf. In Matt.*, hom. 4, as given in S.T. of St Thomas, III, 39, i.

> the Son of God. For God has predestined us to be his adopted sons, he has conformed us to the glorious body of Christ. Henceforth you are participants in Christ and so you are rightly called 'christs'. It was of you that God said 'Touch not my christs' (Psalm 104. 15). You have become christs for you have received the imprint of the Holy Spirit and all the rites that have been carried out on you have been done symbolically (*eikonkōs*) since you are ikons (*eikones*) of Christ.[6]

This image of Christ, this *eikon* of Christ that we are, is not formed all at once. If we accept Christ into our lives it goes on being formed within us until at the end it will shine with the reflected glory of the Son of God, and as we approach the Father it is our prayer that he will look on us with favour as he looked on his Son 'in whom he was well pleased'. When then we celebrate the Baptism of the Lord we should realize that Christ is reaching out to us with power, gradually forming his *eikon* within us, until his light shines more brightly and his life permeates our whole being.

[6] *Catéchèses mystagogiques*, 3.i, p. 121 (ed. A. Piédagnel, Sources chrétiennes, 126, Paris, 1966).

THE TEMPTATION

*

EVEN a superficial reading of the first three gospels reveals that there are differences between Mark's account of the temptation and the accounts found in Matthew and Luke. Mark's is very brief, the Matthaean and Lucan accounts are much longer descriptions of the event and differ from each other but little. Mark simply says that Jesus was in the wilderness and was tempted by Satan. It has been described as an objective account,[1] unconcerned with the subjective dispositions of the tempted. That is evident from the text. But the moral aspect of the Matthaean and Lucan account is contrasted with the Marcan account that has no such concern. The contrast may however not be so great. Jesus is in conflict with the powers of evil and Matthew and Luke present the evil in more detailed and concrete terms than Mark does. What are the solicitations of the Evil One? These are spelt out by Matthew and Luke. What is beyond question is that Jesus experiences evil in his own person for the first time. He was

[1] D. E. Nineham, *St Mark*, The Pelican Gospel Commentaries (1963), pp. 34,63.

engaged in a struggle between good and evil that had been going on since the fall of man. The temptation was the beginning of his own struggle as the Messiah of God, a struggle that would go on throughout his life (hence the exorcisms and the healings) until his death. In the words of the Easter hymn: *Mors et vita duello/conflixere mirando* (death and life were engaged in wondrous strife) and life conquered death in the resurrection. But the struggle goes on in the Church. 'Put on the whole armour of God' said St Paul, '... for we are not contending against flesh and blood but against the principalities, against the powers, against the world rulers of this present darkness, against the spiritual hosts of wickedness in the heavenly places.' Success in the conflict is only possible if we 'put on Christ', if his faith, his righteousness, his gospel, his word 'which is the sword of the spirit', strengthen us inwardly (Ephesians 6.11–17).

Jesus then was not engaged in a purely personal conflict. He was the Second Adam, the representative of the whole human race both past and future. He stood at the end of the history of the people of God in the Old Testament and recapitulated in his own experience the whole of that history. Adam had fallen to the power of Satan and he must be raised up again. Israel had to be led to God and through the captivity in Egypt and their experiences in the wilderness they became the people of God, bound to him by a covenant which was concretized in sacrifice. They were 'tried' and tempted, they fell away again and again but they never entirely forfeited the promises. Thus, for Matthew Jesus was the new Moses and, as his gospel with its five sections suggests, that it is the new law replacing the Torah, so for Mark the wilderness of the temptations is the desert where the people of old were tried and tested. So whether we look back or forward, whether we think of the old Israel or the new, Jesus stands as a summing up both in himself and his own experience. What he did, what he experienced, he did for us and since Christians are united with him by his grace and through membership of the Body of which he is the head, he is with us in temptation and his power is always available to us.

Thus Jesus in his temptation is not *just* an example but our ever present help. The spiritual power by which he overcame the Adversary is the power by which we overcome whatever temptations assail us.

No doubt the example is important and it has been exploited in dozens of spiritual books for centuries but some, especially the perspicacious young, find that the comparison of ourselves with Jesus is unreal. He was the Son of God and the issue was never in doubt. The thought that Jesus is overcoming our temptations with us and within us carries a more powerful message. This the Fathers of the Church kept in view with the exemplary character of Christ's temptation, even if they threw greater emphasis on the latter than the positive help it can give us. St Gregory the Great for instance could say that Christ was tempted to bring us help in our temptations for it was not unfitting that 'our Redeemer should be tempted since he had come to undergo death so that he overcame our temptations by his, just as he triumphed over death by his death'. St Augustine, writing two centuries before, keeps in balance the example and the help: 'If Christ was tempted by Satan it was in view of being our Mediator that we might overcome our temptations not only by his help but also by his example.'[2] It is to be noted that both writers associate the temptation with the redeeming work of Christ. The temptation was an episode in that work; it was the first conflict with the powers of evil whose influence would be gradually quelled by Jesus's teaching, by his miracles of healing and by his exorcisms, all signs of the coming of the Kingdom which Jesus was inaugurating. What he did then continues in the life of the Church, and by his victory over evil we too can overcome.

But it is perhaps St Leo who penetrates most deeply into the meaning of the temptation. He put his teaching in the context of Lent and it would seem that as early as the beginning of the fifth century the gospel of the temptation was read at Mass on the First Sunday of Lent. At the beginning of Lent, he says, we are entering upon a struggle, an *agōn,* against the temptations that come even while we are fasting and engaged in good works, temptations that may well be

[2] Gregory: *Homil. 16 in Evang.*; Augustine, *De Trinitate,* 4.cap. 13; both texts as given in *Summa Theol.* III 41, a.1.

all the stronger since 'the greater the attention we give to our salvation, the more violent will be the attacks of the enemy'. But there is no reason for dismay for '*he who is in us* is stronger than the adversary who is against us, and if we trust in the power of the One within us we shall receive strength through him. For the Lord allowed himself to be tempted that *we might both be fortified by his help and instructed by his example*' (... *ut cuius munimur auxilio, eiusdem erudiremur exemplo*). There can be no doubt about Leo's meaning and his emphasis on the One 'who is in us' is striking. With Christ dwelling in us we can engage in the *agōn* and with him and through him we can overcome. This Leo goes on to underline; 'He fought then that we might fight after him; he conquered then that we also might conquer.'

For Leo our conflict is not only with visible evil in this world, but, as he goes on to quote, 'We are not contending against flesh and blood but against the world rulers of this present darkness, against the spiritual hosts of wickedness in the heavenly places.' Therefore we must put on 'the whole armour of God' and, taking up St Paul's military terms, Leo concludes this part of his sermon with a series of metaphors drawn from the Roman army of the time: 'Look upon the Leader (*dux*), distinguished for his many victories, the unconquered Marshal of the Christian forces (*Christianae militiae magister*), and see the powerful weapons, the insurmountable defences with which he has armed us.' The weapons are those of Ephesians 6 mentioned above but the *Dux* and the *Magister Militum* (a Byzantine term) does not lead from far away but from within the Christian who enters upon the struggle with the powers of evil. If anything is calculated to give the Christian courage it is this and so the example and the help are combined.[3]

If it is asked how Christ's power is mediated to us, St Leo replies: through the keeping of Lent which involves prayer, fasting and alms-giving. These for him are inseparably connected. Fasting is not an exercise in self-regarding mortification, though the radical centripetal tendencies of human nature must be corrected, passions must be controlled and sin repented, but it must always be turned out to those in need. We deprive ourselves of what we have not simply as a matter of self-denial but so that from what we go without we may feed and clothe the hungry and the naked. And neither of these practices is authentic without prayer which is an opening out of the self to God, a listening to his word and a turning to him in petition and repentance. It could probably be going beyond Leo's *expressed* thought to say that the fasting, whether it is simple abstinence or other acts of self-denial, is a fasting with Christ and through that self-identification with him fasting becomes possible and fruitful. Alms-giving likewise is a continuation of

[3] *Sermo* I, iii, *De Quadragesima* (R. Dolle, *Léon le Grand, Sermons*, t.II, pp. 29,30 Sources chrétiennes, 49, Paris 1957). Migne, PL, 54, cc. 265,266.

the self-giving of Christ whose heart went out to the hungry, the possessed, the sick, the sinner and those troubled in mind and spirit. Above all, prayer is with Christ and in Christ through whom we make our prayer to the Father. Thus the traditional 'exercises' of Lent, which can be seen simply as external 'good works', are done in Christ and are fruitful only because they are so done.

But not only is Christ's power mediated through the Lenten observance thus understood. For Leo the celebration of the liturgy of Lent is of central importance. On Sundays and Wednesdays (it would seem) the Christian people met to hear God's word and for Leo, as for us now, in its proclamation Christ is present.[4] Through the word the saving deeds of God throughout the Old Testament and through Christ himself are recalled and in some sense made present.[5] That presence is even more immediate in the eucharist which the Christian people gather together Sunday by Sunday to celebrate. But also with the catechumens and the penitents, who are in the last stages of their preparation, the people return to God through repentance and reconciliation and await the renewal of their baptismal grace in the celebration of the Paschal Feast at Easter. All in fact is directed to 'the greatest feast of all feasts' which the

[4] *Constitution on the Liturgy*, nos. 7,33: 'Christ is present in his word . . . is still proclaiming his Gospel'.

[5] Ibid. no. 102.

whole Church celebrates at Easter. For this, he says, we must prepare by the Lenten observance so that we may die with Christ in his passion, in whose resurrection we are raised up; as St Paul the apostle said: 'You are dead and your life is hidden with Christ in God. When Christ, your life, appears, then you will appear with him in glory' (Colossians 3.3–4).[6]

[6] The phrase 'greatest feast of all feasts' is from Sermo 12 at the beginning (Dolle, pp. 85,86). The rest of the paragraph is dependent on various of the twelve sermons St Leo preached on the First Sunday of Lent. Baptism is referred to several times and reconciliation, often in connection with baptism, rather fewer times. Thus in the sixth sermon we find this: 'It is a special feature of the Paschal Feast that the whole Church rejoices in the remission of sins which is realized not only in those who are reborn in the sacrament of baptism but also in those who are already counted among the adopted children (of God) .... All must make an effort so that on *the day of redemption* none may be found still in the vices of this former (unregenerate) condition' (p. 57). It is not clear that Leo was speaking of the *sacrament* of reconciliation—though it is highly probable, and we do not know whether the public reconciliation of sinners in the first half of the fifth century was celebrated on what we call Maundy Thursday or not. It must have taken place, however, close to Easter.

THE TRANSFIGURATION

*

THE Transfiguration is different from the other events of the gospel, the birth, the baptism, the temptation, that have been considered here. At the birth the heavenly light shone on the shepherds, not on Jesus; at the Epiphany the star was to lead the Magi; and though there was a kind of epiphany at the baptism it was more a theophany, a revelation of the Father and the Holy Spirit. In the temptation the divinity was obscured, even if after the event and in the light of the whole gospel message we can see that the One who was repelling Satan's solicitations was the Son of God. The only comparable events with the Transfiguration were the appearances after the resurrection when the apostles were again struck with awe.

Jesus' body was transfigured and the mysterious light that permeated his whole being shone through his clothes: 'and he was transfigured before them', namely Peter, James and John. Mark speaks of the clothes: 'his garments became glistening, intensely white, as no fuller on earth could bleach them' (Mark 9.2,3). To this Matthew adds: 'his *face* shone like the sun and his garments became white as light' (Matthew 17.2), which reminds us of the vision in the

Revelation of St John, 'his head and his hair were white as wool, white as snow and his eyes were like a flame of fire' (1.14). It is as though those who handed on the tradition hardly knew how to describe the manifestation; 'for he (Peter) did not know what to say'. This is not surprising; the disciples were filled with awe and the event was unique. Perhaps they or those who heard their message remembered the story of Moses coming down from mount Sinai; his face shone so that no one could look at it. He had been talking with God (Exodus 34.7). And they seem to have recalled Elijah going up to heaven in a chariot of fire drawn by fiery horses (2 Kings 1.11). Both men had experienced God, Moses on the mountain and Elijah in the stillness after the storm (1 Kings 19.14). Both were 'seers' of God, both were prophets; Moses had to lead the people through trial and suffering to the Promised Land and Elijah had to bring the people of his time back to God, back to repentance. They were the fitting companions of Jesus in his transfiguration. All this would have been in the minds of the disciples and of those who later listened to them, and it was perhaps in this way that they came to terms with their extraordinary experience.

The gospel of the Transfiguration has been read on the Second Sunday of Lent since the time of St Leo in the fifth century and this has suggested his interpretation of the event: it was to strengthen the disciple's faith before the passion and the death. This too seems to have been in the mind of the writers of the synoptic gospels for all three set it in the context of the passion, death and resurrection of Christ: 'As they were coming down from the mountain, he charged them to tell no one what they had seen, until the Son of Man should have risen from the dead' (Mark 9.9). For St Luke it was the beginning of his 'departure', his *exodos*, his going up to Jerusalem where he would suffer, die and rise again (9.31). The Transfiguration was a preparation of the disciples for the ignominy of the passion and the death on the cross, and a foreshadowing of Christ's rising from the dead though they did not understand what this meant (Mark 9.10).

This then is how Leo treats the subject:

> In the transfiguration it was Christ's principal intent to remove from the disciples' hearts the scandal of the cross, so that their faith should not be disturbed by the sight of his suffering—suffering freely accepted—once they had seen the eminence of his dignity, hitherto hidden from them.

But that reference to the resurrection in the gospel accounts suggests another line of thought. Although he is not explicit about the matter, St Leo's thought seems to move on to the resurrection, the definitive epiphany and transfiguration of Jesus, when the new life of the Risen Christ will make those who believe in him sons and daughters of God. What the Transfiguration holds out in promise will then be fulfilled:

> But not less providentially the hope of holy Church was founded, for the whole body could recognize how great was the gift by which it was to be transformed: to its members was promised a share of the glory that now shone in the Head. Of this the Lord spoke when referring to his coming glory: 'Then the righteous will shine like the sun in the kingdom of their Father' (Matthew 13.43).

To this he adds the message of St Paul in Romans 8.18–21: 'I consider the sufferings of this present time not worth comparing with the glory that is to be revealed to us ...' and he backs this up with Colossians 3.3,4: 'For you have died and your life is hid with Christ in God. When Christ our life appears, then you also will appear with him in glory.' But this statement is in an Easter-baptismal context (2.12,20) and the first reference must be to the resurrection and its effects in the life of the followers of Christ. St Paul in fact goes on to say how the new Christians are to live.

But both in St Paul (Colossians 3.4), and, it would seem, in the Transfiguration, there is an eschatological dimension. The Transfiguration is not only a revelation to strengthen the disciples' faith; it holds out a promise, the promise that through their faithfulness Christians who are in Christ will enter into the kingdom of the glorious Christ at the end of time. If this is so, it is not surprising; resurrection and the consummation at the end of time are not so sharply distinguished in the New Testament. For St

John the disciples had already beheld the glory: 'We have beheld his glory, glory of the only Son from the Father' (John 1.14) and, *pace* those who hold a 'realized eschatology', John's vision goes beyond the 'glory' of the cross to an indeterminate future, to, as I believe, the Last Times when all who are 'in Christ' will then behold his glory: 'Father, I desire that they also whom thou hast given me, may be with me where I am, to behold my glory which thou hast given me in thy love before the foundation of the world' (17.24).

The immediate perspective however is the celebration of the passion, the death and the resurrection, that is the paschal mystery, at Easter. For St Leo Lent was a preparation by prayer, fasting and alms-giving for that event. He called the whole Christian community in Rome to make that preparation and among them were the catechumens, although he does not mention them. But doubtless the reason for the inclusion of this gospel passage on the Second Sunday of Lent was that now they were in the period of 'enlightenment'. On the First Sunday of Lent the candidates were (and still are) solemnly enrolled as catechumens. Now they would meet Christ in his word, now they would be led into an ever deeper understanding of Christ to whom they would commit themselves definitely in the celebration of the paschal sacraments of baptism (itself called 'enlightenment'), confirmation and the holy eucharist. To make this journey or pilgrimage they were urged to put away once and for all anything that held them earth-bound and the Christian community were called to accompany them. All looked forward to the end when through sharing in the passion, death and resurrection of Christ the catechumens would be initiated into his life and that life would be renewed within the Christians.

It is understandable then that Lent was regarded as a struggle, an *agōn*, which, strenuous as it might be, was undertaken in the Christ who had experienced the *agōn* in the Temptation as he would the *agōn* of the Garden; his victory to be revealed in the resurrection. Taking up the words of the gospel Leo elaborates as follows:

> Listen to him who opens the way to heaven and who through the torment of the cross prepares for you a step by which you may ascend to the kingdom. Why does redemption make you tremble? Why do you fear to be delivered from your wound? Let your willing be enfolded in Christ's will. Cast off fear and arm yourself with steadfast faith. It is not fitting that you should fear in the passion of the Saviour what by his grace you will have no reason to fear at the end.

Leo then takes up again his first theme of faith. He sees the apostles as representing the whole Church which in its turn needs to be strengthened by the deepening of its faith in the redeeming Christ. He then returns to the theme of the passion which he sees as the source of strength by which we may suffer in Christ and so come to the glory that is promised us:

May the preaching of the gospel confirm the faith of everyone. Let no one be ashamed of the cross of Christ by which the world was redeemed. Let no one be afraid who suffers for righteousness, let no one despair of the reward that has been promised. For we pass from toil to rest, from death to life, since he took upon himself all our weakness, all our lowliness, and if we persevere in faith in him and in love of him, *we shall conquer because he has conquered* and what he promised we receive. So, whether in keeping his commandments or suffering adversity the voice of the Father should always resound in our ears: 'This is my beloved Son with whom I am well pleased; listen to him.'

If we look at the collect for the Feast of the Transfiguration on 6th August we find that though it is a late composition and hardly classical in form, it resumes much of the traditional doctrine.

In the first member of the first sentence we find the phrase *fidei sacramenta*, the sacraments of faith. These are said to be 'confirmed' by the witness of the 'fathers', Moses and Elijah, appearing at the Transfiguration. What are the 'sacraments of faith' that are confirmed? For St Leo and no doubt for other patristic writers they are the signs, types and foreshadowings in the Old Testament of what will happen in the New. These are termed variously *signa, mysteria, sacramenta* and it is these that are now being confirmed because they are seen to be fulfilled in Christ. The reflection of the divine glory that had shone on the face of Moses and the fire that swept Elijah to heaven is now the light of glory shining 'on the face of Jesus Christ'. Both bore witness to the reality that had now come. But in the patristic tradition the 'sacraments of faith' were not confined to types and shadows; they were the 'mysteria' of Christ's life which are celebrated and made present to the Church now. And the heart of these mysteries was the paschal mystery of the suffering, the death and the resurrection through which the 'work of our redemption' was accomplished. The vision of Christ in glory as it is celebrated in the liturgy is the confirming of these mysteries and the pledge that the adopted children of the Father, co-heirs with Christ, will share in the enlightenment of baptism and in his glory at the end. But, as Leo says, they must persevere in faith and love.

This too is the message of the Preface of the feast when we give thanks that 'the whole body of Christ will one day share in the glory that once shone in the Head'.

The Transfiguration then is not simply a past event. Through the liturgy its reality is conveyed to us, though it will take time, a whole life, before 'the riches of the glory of this mystery, which is Christ in you' becomes not merely a hope but an eternal reality (Colossians 1.17).

Note:
The feast of the Transfiguration was not inserted into the Roman Calendar until 1456 but in the Byzantine Liturgy, where it was known as early as the sixth century, it is one of the greatest feasts. In the West, Peter the Venerable, Abbot of Cluny, did much to propagate it in the twelfth century.

The Byzantine feast does much to show the relationship with the passion and the glory of the cross. It is related to the feast of the Exaltation of the Cross and certain chants from the liturgy, called *catavasia*, are used for Mattins of the Transfiguration and in various and usually typological ways refer to the cross. See P. F. Mercenier and F. Paris, *La Prière des Eglises de rite byzantin*, Amay-sur-Meuse, Belgium, 1939, t II, i.p.282.

For the history of the feast see *L'Eglise en Prière*, ed. A. G. Martimort, new edition, t.IV, pp. 112–113.

For St Leo see Sermo LI as in Migne's *Patrologia Latins*, t.54, coll. 308–313, sections iii, vii, viii.

THE PRAYER

*

THAT Christ prayed is so evident in the gospel accounts that there is no need to detail all the occasions when he is found doing so. But there are cetain prayers which he uttered that deserve attention since they indicate the attitude we should have if we would pray 'in Christ'. The most striking in the synoptists is his prayer found in Matthew 11.25–28 (*par.* Luke 10.21–22):

> I thank thee, Father, Lord of heaven and earth, that thou hast hidden these things from the wise and understanding and revealed them to babes; yea, Father, for such was thy gracious will. All things have been delivered to me by my Father; and no one knows the Son except the Father and no one knows the Father except the Son and any one to whom the Son chooses to reveal him.

Much has been written about this passage, which has been described as a meteorite falling from the Johannine heaven, because it seems so unlike anything in the synoptists. Certainly it is one of the most sublime statements in all four gospels and in the strictest sense of the word it is a revelation. It is a revelation of the intimate relationship of the Father to the Son and the Son to the Father for that word 'know' means, in biblical terms, much more than mere knowledge. It means a living, intimate relationship of union, a knowing that is transfused with love. It is significant that Jesus felt the need to express it, and to express it in prayer for we may suppose that throughout his life he was conscious of this union. The prayer had become a necessity though it is difficult to discern from the gospel accounts what prompted it.[1]

This sense of intimacy is revealed in the word 'Father' under which, almost certainly, lies the Aramaic word 'Abba'—which is described as an intimate expression, though with a suggestion of reverence, used by a child to his father. Furthermore, it is unique to Jesus, for 'there is no single instance of God being addressed as Abba in the literature of Jewish Prayer'.[2] This word alone then expresses that intimacy and is paralleled by the numerous instances when Jesus refers to the Father, but always in relation to himself as 'my Father and your Father'. This too is sufficient to suggest the fundamental attitude of the Christian who would pray in Christ. We are children of God by baptism and we are children in the Child—a favourite term for Jesus (*pais*) in early

[1] In Matthew the incident comes between the condemnation of Chorazin and Bethsaida, and the rebuke of the Pharisees to the disciples for plucking ears of wheat on the Sabbath.

[2] See J. J. Jeremias, *The Prayers of Jesus* (1967), p. 57.

Christian literature—or as a modern theologian has put it, we are *filii in Filio*, sons in the Son, and when we pray we are praying in Christ.

We need also to note the verb 'I thank', differently translated in different versions (e.g. 'I bless'), because it is used both of 'blessing' God and of thanking him or indeed of 'confessing' to him, which may mean praising God, as in the psalms, or confessing sin to him, which was the term in the second century for the rite of penance (*exomologesis*). Broadly speaking, it signifies a mingling of praise, blessing and thanksgiving which is drawn from Jesus as he expresses his awareness of the glory of his Father and of his union with him. It is certainly an out-going of himself to his Father, perhaps a sort of 'ecstasy', (*ek-stasis*), and we may reasonably suppose that in this prayer Jesus was expressing what was the invariable undertow of his life, the very meaning of his existence and mission (cf John 4.34 'My food is to do the will of him who sent me'; and cf 5.30; 6.38–40). In this prayer he is saying that he is totally given to the Father, as is made explicit in the prayer of John 17.19: 'And for their (the disciples') sake I consecrate myself' or 'dedicate myself' to the total giving of himself on the cross.

The next phrase to which we might turn is 'thou hast hidden these things from the wise and understanding and revealed them to babes'. What is being revealed comes in the next verse; only those receive it who are 'babes', the little ones, the 'poor ones' of the last ages of the Old Testament; to 'the wise and understanding', those who 'know', the revelation is hidden. Why, we may ask? The 'understanding', those who 'know' (or perhaps the 'know-alls') are probably the Pharisees and the scribes who were learned in the Law, and the 'wise' may be those who are wise in the wisdom of this world (cf 1 Corinthians 1.19); in any case those whose minds are shut. On the other hand, the little ones were the *anawim* among whom are to be included Mary and Joseph and Simeon who, inspired by the Holy Spirit, recognized the Saviour who lay in his arms. The inference then is that in prayer we must have our hearts open to the word of Jesus and the inspiration of the Holy Spirit if we would share in the relationship Jesus has with the Father, for only then shall we be counted among those to whom Jesus chooses to reveal him. Jesus shows that he is totally open to the Father whose love embraced him who is his Son, the Chosen One. We too are chosen in Christ (Ephesians 1.4), we too are in the Son upon whom the Father's favour rests and in consequence, if we are united with him, that favour rests on us too.

This prayer is paralleled by one we find in John 11.42: 'Father, I thank thee that thou hast heard me. I knew that thou hearest me always, but I have said this on account of the people standing by, that they may believe that thou didst send me.' Although Jesus was deeply moved by the death of his friend Lazarus, here there is a great calm and assurance. He is confident that his Father always hears him, he is at one with his

Father, he is, we may suppose, in unbroken communion with his Father and what he asks will certainly be granted precisely because his will is one with his Father's; he came to do the will of the Father who sent him. The message is clear: it is only if our will is united with the will of Jesus that our prayer can be answered but if it is so united, it certainly will be. 'Ask and it will be given you' said Jesus, 'seek and you will find; knock and it will be opened to you. For every one who asks receives, and he who seeks finds, and to him who knocks it will be opened' (Luke 11.9–10). There are no reservations here. To ask in faith and with submission to God's will means that our prayer will be answered. John simply makes explicit the condition that underlies all Christian prayer: 'If you abide in me, and my words abide in you, ask whatever you will, and it shall be done to you' (John 15.7; and cf 15.16; 14.13).

But nothing reveals more clearly the identity of Jesus' will with that of his Father than the prayer in the garden before his death. It shows that the relationship with his Father was real, personal and not merely 'theological'. In Mark the word 'Abba' is actually used (14.36) and the total dependence and submission of the Son to the Father is revealed precisely in the work of salvation that he was bringing about. Finally and more important than all else, the reality of the relationship is revealed by the struggle, in traditional language the *agony*, that submission to the will of the Father demanded of him

(John 12.27). Jesus was always Son and he realized this existentially in the experience of his life. He was *conscious* of his Sonship and it was the most precious thing in his life. Nothing must be allowed to interfere with it and when Jesus so ruthlessly repelled Peter ('Get behind me, Satan', Matthew 17.23) it was because Peter was in danger of running against the will of the Father for the salvation of mankind to be effected by his Son through suffering.[2]

Whether John 17.1–26 was written up by John himself or the final editor of the gospel,[3] the writer was extraordinarily faithful to what we know of Jesus' prayer in other places. God is to be glorified by the *exodos* of the Son through suffering, death and in the resurrection when the glory that was his from the beginning, before the world was made, will shine out from him as he achieves the status of the Risen Christ. Jesus has done his Father's will or is doing it, he has accomplished the work the Father gave him to do. Since his disciples have received his word, which is the word of the Father, they are his but he prays that they may be kept, guarded, 'in thy name' that 'they may be one even as we are one'. The prayer is for union, the union of the disciples with Christ through which they will enter into union with the Father. That this may be so, they are to be preserved from the

[2] See J. J. Jeremias, *The Prayers of Jesus* (1967), p. 57.

[3] See Raymond E. Brown, *The Gospel according to St John*, two vols. (1966, 1971).

Evil One (cf the Lord's prayer) but more fundamentally union is the fruit of love: 'I in them and thou in me, that the world may know that thou has sent me and hast loved them *even* as thou hast loved me.' Then if they remain in him, if they are one as he and the Father are one, 'the world will believe that thou hast sent me'. The kingdom will come through those who believe, who are united by love and bear that love to the world. On the eve of his redeeming death Jesus consecrates or dedicates himself to God's work and the disciples too are to be consecrated to the 'truth' which is the Word, Christ himself. This 'truth' they will manifest to the world, they will proclaim it and through others who come after them it will go on being preached until the kingdom has come completely and in effect. Then the disciples and all who followed them and all who have proclaimed the Truth will enter into the glory: 'Father, I desire that they also ... may be with me where I am, to behold my glory which thou hast given me in thy love for me before the foundation of the world.'

The glorifying of the Father, the hallowing of the Name,[4] the prayer for the kingdom and the doing of the Father's will are all found here. The doing of God's will is expressed in John by the word union; union with God in and through Christ is the indispensable condition of doing the work of God and of prayer to him. This is the guarantee that the

[4] The verb for 'consecrate' and 'hallow' in Greek is the same.

world will believe that God sent his Son into the world so that eventually all will be united to him and through him to the Father. *Then* there will be one flock and one shepherd.

Throughout the ages, Christian writers and theologians have asked why Jesus prayed and the answer comes again and again: to give us an example. Although that reason is suggested in two places in St John's gospel (11.24; 12.27–30), it is not mentioned elsewhere. Jesus withdraws for private prayer (Mark 2.35). According to Luke he prayed before choosing the apostles (6.12), he was praying before Peter made his confession of faith to him (9.18–20), he prayed before the Transfiguration (9.28), he was praying before giving his disciples the Lord's prayer (and here his example seems to have caught their attention) and, as is recorded in Mark and Matthew, he prayed before his passion. He prayed on the cross and his prayer seems to have been torn out of him by the necessity of the occasion. Whatever the theological complexities, there can be little doubt that Jesus felt the need to pray, especially in his agony when he asked his Father to forgive his executioners, and, in the extremity of his suffering, he voiced his prayer in the words of psalm 21 (22). His prayer, all his prayer, was a genuine outpouring of his soul.

Like the beatitudes the Lord's prayer is the reflection of his life. He had come to give glory to his Father, his very life was to do the will of his Father and had for its aim the bringing in of the kingdom, the reign of his Father. He lived from day to day, without anywhere to lay his head and dependent on what others gave him. In the supreme test (temptation) of his life he prayed to be delivered from it—but always in accordance with his Father's will.

Perhaps it would be better then to say that the prayer of Jesus is not so much an example as a *model.* Just as we are exhorted to the 'imitation of Christ' in our living, so we 'imitate' him in our prayer. But that does not mean mere copying. In a much misunderstood saying, the artist 'imitates' nature not in the sense that he produces photographic replicas of what he sees around him (the camera can do that much better) but in the sense that he scrutinizes or even contemplates nature, trying to understand its inner reality and working according to its inbuilt laws. He seeks to understand stone as it were from within so that he may carve from it an object that is in accordance with the nature of stone. He knows that he cannot do with stone what he would do with paint. Likewise, our imitation of Christ must come from a faith-knowledge of him, a knowledge which is the fruit of contemplation. The Christian in his life and in his prayer strives to enter into Christ and to become aware that he is in fact in Christ through the operation of the Holy Spirit who is given to him.

So important is this praying in Christ that St Paul sees it as possible only by the intervention of the Holy Spirit:

You have received the spirit of sonship. When we cry,

> "Abba, Father!" it is the Spirit himself bearing witness with our spirit that we are children of God, and if children then heirs, heirs of God and fellow heirs with Christ, provided we suffer with him in order that we may also be glorified with him (Romans 8.15–16 and cf Galatians 4.6).

Just as we can only say 'Jesus is Lord' by the Holy Spirit, so we can only call upon the Father, Abba, as Jesus did because the Spirit is with us, with us in our prayer, prompting our prayer even when we are unaware of his presence:

> Likewise the Spirit helps us in our weakness; for we do not know how to pray as we ought, but the Spirit himself intercedes for us with sighs too deep for words. And he who searches the hearts of men knows what is the mind of the Spirit, because the Spirit intercedes for the saints according to the will of God (Romans 8.26–27).[5]

The Spirit is with us in our prayer, becoming as it were the mind of our prayer so that the Father who searches all hearts recognizes in it 'the mind of the Spirit'. What is more, we can say that it is he who returns our prayer through Christ to the Father so that prayer at its deepest 'is shown to be not merely a saying of words but a kind of living in God'.[6] This is how St Augustine saw things. For him 'prayer is the

[5] The root verb 'intercedes' is the same here as in Hebrews 7.25 where Christ is said to be always living to intercede for us.

[6] See *Christian Celebration: The Prayer of the Church,* p. 18.

expression of the desire for God who has revealed himself ... It is as it were the ground-base of the Christian's life'. It is in this way that we can pray as the scriptures say 'without ceasing' for although we feel impelled to express our desire in words, that longing for God, prompted by the Holy Spirit, can continue even when words are not used.[7] In a word, prayer is a permanent way of living, we are turned towards God in deeds, in work, in all we do, and it erupts, so to say, when at the prompting of the Spirit we give utterance to what we *are* or try to be in words.

Against this background we can see the deep implications of praying the Lord's prayer. First, we are putting ourselves with Christ; as he was Son by nature, we are the Father's children through him. As his prayer went out first to the Father in praise and thanksgiving, so does ours when we say 'Our Father in heaven, hallowed be thy name'. As his 'work' was to bring in the kingdom, so we pray that the reign of God may penetrate more fully into every part of human existence. His 'food' was to do the will of his Father who sent him and we ask that our will may be enclosed in his so that we may will what he wills. Thus united in the depths of our being with him we can confidently ask the Father for our 'daily bread', for all the needs of our life and for the needs of others. The forgiveness we ask for ourselves comes through his eternal pleading (Hebrews 7.25) and the

[7] *Ibid.* p. 19.

forgiveness we extend to others is only possible through the saving mercy he communicates to us. As he faced and overcame in the test he experienced in the wilderness and in the final test of the passion and his death, so we may overcome whatever tests or tempts us in this life, and with a sure confidence we can hope to be victorious through and with him in the final test of our death. As in his life and death he was in conflict with evil, withdrawing its sting, so we pray that his power will overcome evil whether it is in ourselves or comes to us from outside. When then we pray the Lord's prayer we need to put ourselves in the posture of Christ. Like him we are, or try to be, completely submissive to the Father's will and with unshaken trust we ask for what we need, for our prayer is united with him who is ever-living to make intercession for us (Hebrews 7.25).

But we also pray in the Spirit, who, as St Paul has said, dwells in the depths of our being, enabling us to call out to the Father through Jesus Christ. As a seventeenth century writer has put it:

> By grace the Holy Spirit is poured into our hearts where the Father ceaselessly begets him by an uninterrupted operation, as long as we persevere in holiness. There he forms one voice (with us), not now as His Spirit but as the Spirit of our spirit; not now as the Spirit of the Head but as the Spirit of the Head-in-the members. He does not cry for himself; he cries both for us and in us, as if he were but one thing, but one mystical person, with us. And as he is but one life with us, *he is also but one voice with*

> *us. It is he who cries and prays in us* and by consequence he is the source of every supernatural operation (within us).[8]

It is as if our prayer were tranfused by the prayer of the Holy Spirit who voices our prayer and through Christ returns it to the Father. It is perhaps not too much to say that our voice in prayer enters into the intimate life of the Trinity and is mingled with the perpetual giving and receiving of love that is the life of the Godhead. Prayer is living, a living in God himself.

Christian prayer, all Christian prayer, is 'in Christ' who gives us the Holy Spirit, the life-force or dynamism of that prayer. And if this is true of prayer in general, it is particularly true of liturgical prayer, the Prayer of the Church, for 'Christ is present when the Church prays and sings, for he promised "Where two or three are gathered together in my name, there I am in the midst of them" (Matthew 18.20)'.[9] The basic movement of that prayer is to the Father through the Son and in the Holy Spirit. As the Constitution on the Liturgy says '"The victory and the triumph of his (Christ's) death are again made present" and at the same time thanks are given to God "for his unspeakable gift" in Jesus Christ, "in praise of his glorious grace which he freely bestowed

[8] Louis Chardon, *La Croix de Jesus,* 1647. I have used the edition of 1894/5, t. I, p. 31. Italics and words in brackets have been added by me.

[9] Constitution on the Liturgy, para. 7.

on us in the Beloved", through the power of the Holy Spirit.'[10] As we pray in the Third Eucharistic Prayer 'Grant, (Father), that we who are nourished by his body and blood, may be filled with his Holy Spirit and become one body, one spirit in Christ.'

[10] *Ibid.* para. 6; scripture references 2 Corinthians 9.15; Ephesians 1.12.

THE HEALING

*

THE miracles of Jesus have conventionally been regarded as proofs of his divinity. This is not quite the gospel perspective. In the synoptists they are acts of power showing that the reign (kingdom) of God is coming. They indicate indeed that in Jesus Christ the reign of God is beginning. In the synoptic gospels

> the miracles are primarily acts of power (*dynameis*) accompanying the breaking of the reign of God into time. The miracles worked by Jesus are not simply proofs of his claims, but more fundamentally are acts by which he establishes God's reign and defeats the reign of Satan. Many of the miracles attack Satan directly by driving out demons. Many more heal sickness which is associated with sin and evil. The raising of men to life is an assault on death which is Satan's peculiar realm. Even nature miracles, like the calming of the storm, are an attack on the disorders introduced into nature by Satan.[1]

To this must be added another dimension. It is not always remembered that Jesus was part of salvation

[1] R. E. Brown, *The Gospel according to St John*, (1966) Vol. I, Appendix iii, p. 525 whence further material below is derived.

history, its culmination, and his redeeming work reached back into the past and inaugurated the messianic age of the future. What he was doing was the continuation of the work of God for the people of the Old Testament. This is clear from his answer to John the Baptist's messengers who asked whether Jesus was the one to come or whether they should look for another (Luke 7.18–22). The reply was twofold: first, there was the work of God: 'In that hour he cured many of diseases and plagues and evil spirits and on many that were blind he bestowed sight'; secondly, there was the word, a quotation from the Old Testament: 'Go and tell John what you have seen and heard: the blind receive their sight, the lame walk, lepers are cleansed, and the deaf hear, the dead are raised up, the poor have the good news preached to them' (cf Isaiah, 35. 5–6; 61.1). Like Jahweh in the Old Testament he is caring for the people, binding up their wounds, strengthening the weak and feeding the flock (cf Ezekiel 34.15–16). His works and his words are signs that he is the Messiah long foretold.

But his miracles can also look on to the future. Especially in John's gospel the Feeding of the Five Thousand, which refers explicitly to the Manna in the desert and looks back to the Exodus experience, also looks on to the eucharistic meal which will be the centre of the Church's life. The withering of the fig tree (Mark 11. 12–14; 20–21), if indeed it was a miracle, foreshadows the rejection of Israel. The miracles of healing may also have a reference to the future: 'The healing of the sick and the raising of the dead may have a secondary symbolism of fulfilling the Old Testament prophetic picture of the day when the Lord would comfort his people by giving life to the dead, sight to the blind etc.'[2]

One or two other incidents, for example the healing of the Canaanite woman's daughter (Matthew 15.21–28), foreshadow the preaching of the gospel to the Gentiles with the implication that they too will benefit from the healing action of God.

In St John's gospel it is plain that miracles are *signs* which point to something beyond themselves, to the 'work' of Jesus, that is his redeeming work for which he came into the world. As a modern commentator has put it, 'It is not that the miracles legitimate Jesus, as though he were some Hellenistic mircle-worker in need of legitimation. Rather, the miracles themselves need legitimation or explanation and this is what the Old Testament supplies.'[3] This is the meaning of Matthew's use of the Isaian texts which he inserts into the gospel story.

If, however, we kept to Matthew's accounts we should miss an important aspect of Jesus' miracles. Jesus loved people, he wished to be of service to them, he had come to serve and not to be served and

[2] *Op. cit.*, p. 526: cf Isaiah, 25,35,61.

[3] John P. Meier, *Matthew* (New Testament Message, Vol. 3, Veritas, Dublin; Glazier, Wilmington Delaware USA, 1980), p. 86.

the people who crowded round him touched his heart. He was 'moved with pity' when a leper approached him (Mark 1.41), he was moved with pity when he saw the young man of Nain, 'the only son of his mother', who was being carried out for burial (Luke 7.13). That expression in Greek is a very strong one. It means that his heart (as we should say), his whole inner being, was moved with pity and it was this that drove him to heal the one and raise the other to life. The same word is used when he feeds the five thousand: 'I have compassion on the crowd' and he did not want them to go away hungry (Mark 8.2). This is particularly significant in this context because in all four gospels the Feeding of the Five Thousand is highly symbolical. It is a foreshadowing of the eucharist and of the eternal banquet when all are called to the wedding feast (Apoc. 19.9). Even so, it is the hunger of the people that prompts Jesus' action. And in the raising of Jairus's daughter his gentle humanity is apparent; he alone remembered that after several days illness she would be hungry (Mark 5.43). Jesus was utterly, profoundly human as he showed when he wept before the tomb of his friend Lazarus and moved others so much that they said, 'See how he loved him'. This is all the more impressive as the miracle was a symbol or acted parable of his own resurrection.

Yet if we look again at Matthew's accounts we find that this element is not wanting. He concludes his accounts of the healing of the leper, the centurion's servant and Peter's mother-in-law with a quotation from Isaiah (53.4): 'He took (or took away) our infirmities and bore our diseases'. This he did by healing the sick and feeding the hungry and although it is not in the perspective of Matthew here, Jesus identified himself with the hungry, the thirsty, the naked and the sick for 'As you did it to one of the least of my people, you did it to me'- (Matthew 25.31–40). The hungry, the thirsty, the naked and the sick are in Christ, one is inclined to say in him by virtue of their suffering so that Pascal could say 'Jesus will be in agony until the end of the world'. It is this understanding of things that impels a Mother Teresa, as it has impelled so many throughout the centuries, to care for the sick and the dying. Christ is in them, whether they know it or not, Christ is with them bearing them up in their sufferings, and as he was compassionate when in direct contact with the people of Palestine, so he extends his pity and his love to those who suffer now. But as Jesus loved people, so Christians when they serve the sick do not love them the less because they love them in Christ. Rather, they love them all the more. Their love is purified, they are made more selfless by Christ's indwelling in them and by their prayer they become more single-minded in their service.

These considerations suggest the answer to the question: Did Jesus come to heal *bodies*? Was he not rather concerned with 'souls' and saving them from sin? If it is suggested that this is a dilemma it is a false one. For far too long we have attempted to divide soul from body, almost as if they were two separate realities that happen to be living together. In the Bible there is no such sharp distinction. 'They shall be two in one flesh': when Adam said of Eve 'This at last is bone from my bones and flesh from my flesh' he was welcoming her as another *person*, equal to himself, one with whom he could enter into a covenant of love that is called marriage (Genesis 2.24). 'Flesh' and 'soul' and 'spirit' are one and if we can, as we do, mentally distinguish 'soul' from 'body', they do not exist apart. The body is an expression of the person and the soul is an expression of the person or rather both together are and both combine to effect whatever human beings do. Since then there is this indivisible entity we call a person it is understandable that in biblical thought sin and sickness are closely associated. The sickness of Job seemed to his friends to be a sign of his sinfulness, a view he indignantly repudiated, a view that Ezekiel was concerned to correct and that Jesus himself rejected: 'Rabbi, who sinned, this man or his parents, that he was born blind? Jesus answered, "It was not that this man sinned, or his parents"' (John 9.2).

In any case as we know now, rather better than our forefathers, the reactions of soul on body and body on soul are much more subtle than they once seemed. A bodily disorder often affects our mental condition and illnesses of the mind can have catastrophic effects on the body. Jesus came to save *people* and saw that sin and sickness often go together. He forgave the sins of the paralyzed man and then healed him (Mark 2.1–12), and to the sick man at the Pool of Bezatha he said after healing him, 'Sin no more, that nothing worse befall you' (John 5.14). Jesus was concerned for the human person and it was this that he would make whole. His love and his power were directed to the body as well as to the soul and healing sicknesses was as much part of his mission as the deliverance of people from sin.

This is the view of the Order for the Anointing of the Sick:

> They (Christians) know that Christ, who during his life often visited and healed the sick, loves them in their illness. Although closely linked with the human condition, sickness cannot as a general rule be regarded as a punishment inflicted on each individual for personal sins (see John 9.3). Christ himself, who is without sin, in fulfilling the words of Isaiah took on all the wounds of his passion and shared in all human pain (see Isaiah 53.4–5). Christ is still pained and tormented in his members, made like him ....

Rightly then we should resist illness, and doctors and those who care for the sick

> should consider it their duty to use all the means which in their judgement may help the sick both physically and spiritually. In doing so they are fulfilling the command of Christ to visit the sick, for Christ implied that those

who visit the sick should be concerned for *the whole person* and offer both physical relief and spiritual comfort.[4]

Jesus, then, exercised a ministry of healing and it would seem that he did not intend it to end with himself. When he sent out the twelve on their trial mission he 'gave them authority over the unclean spirits... And they cast out many demons, and anointed with oil many that were sick and healed them' (Mark 6.7,13). The ministry was in fact continued in the Church, as the Acts of the Apostles records. Not to mention the raising of Dorcas to life (10.36–41), four miracles are attributed to Peter (the first to Peter and John, 3.1–8, called 'a notable sign', 4.16) and several in one of Luke's summaries (5.15) where people thought that even if only the shadow of Peter fell on the sick, they would be healed. Whether in Luke's accounts there was any conscious imitation of the gospel miracles is not clear. The healing of the paralytic which might seem to be very like Mark 2.1–11 shows considerable differences. Peter says to him 'Aeneas, Jesus Christ heals you. Rise and make your bed.'[5] There is no forgiveness of sins and of course it is Jesus who heals and not Peter. This makes it clear that Jesus was continuing his ministry of

[4] *Pastoral Care of the Sick* (Geoffrey Chapman, 1983), pp. 10,11. ICEL translation, Nos. 1,2,4. of General Instruction. Italics added.

[5] Or with *JB*, 'fold up your bed' (Acts 9.34) which is more understandable.

healing through those he had appointed as his apostles.

Four miracles are also recorded of Paul; there is the healing of the lame man, Acts 14.8–11, when the apostle says simply 'Stand upright on your feet' and there is the extraordinary incident of the people carrying away handkerchiefs and aprons that had touched Paul and applying them to their sick. It is rather like the use of relics later on. Finally, there is the exorcism of the girl 'soothsayer' and the raising of Eutychus who fell out of the window overcome by heat and the length of Paul's sermon (16.16–18; 20.9–10). All these incidents are recorded laconically and Luke makes no attempt to relate them to the healing ministry of Christ. But that they were so cannot be doubted.

If the Letter of St James was written before AD 62, as seems possible, it witnesses to the practice of the apostolic church and perhaps to the apostles themselves. Mark 6.7–13 is not so far away. That the rite recorded in James 5.14–15 is an act of the Church is shown by the presence of the 'elders', presbyters (cf 1 Timothy 5.17–18; 4.14; Titus 1.5) who pray over the sick man and anoint him with oil '*in the name of the Lord*'. Here is a direct reference to Jesus' ministry of healing. As a result the man will be raised up, 'saved', that is, restored to health. But his sins will also be forgiven and thus the spiritual and physical healing are brought together. The whole human person is healed by the power of Christ mediated through the rite that the Church came to call the Sacrament of Anointing.

Its history can be traced with some difficulty through the suceeding centuries, through Hippolytus who in the early third century speaks of the people bringing their vessels of oil to be blessed at the end of the eucharistic prayer, through Pope Innocent I (417) who orders that the oil should be chrism, to the early Roman books of the sixth and seventh centuries which provide prayers for the blessing of the oil. Later on the Anointing of the Sick began to be associated with reconciliation before death and for long was regarded as the sacrament to prepare a person for death. This was corrected by the Order for the Anointing of the Sick which was issued in 1972.

The document, which is called the *Pastoral Care and the Anointing of the Sick*, sets out the whole ministry of healing from which I will select only one or two points.[6]

In this Order the Church urges lay-people to care for the sick and it provides material to help in this matter. Readings, psalms, and other prayers are suggested. If it is a priest who visits he will lay his hand on the head of the sick person after giving a blessing. Anyone else, deacon or lay-person, is not supposed to lay on hands but, as in charismatic circles, there would seem to be no reason why they should not do so. No doubt as a minister of Christ the

[6] See my *Christian Celebration* (1981), pp. 168–191.

priest has a special role to play. In the liturgy he represents Christ and continues Christ's ministry sacramentally. His laying-on of hands can be seen as the continuation of Christ's gesture, but all baptized lay-people share in the priestly office of Christ and at their own level may lay hands on a sick fellow-Christian, praying that Christ will heal the sick person if that is God's will. The gesture however achieves its full significance in the Sacrament of Anointing when, after a litany of intercession, the priest lays hands on the sick person in silence. Then after another prayer of thanksgiving (or blessing) over the oil he anoints the sick person. Acting in the name of Christ and praying over the sick person, the priest continues the gesture of Christ and anoints as the Lord bade his disciples to do.

The care of the sick normally includes the giving of Holy Communion and since it is usually given many times in the course of a single illness one is prompted to ask if it too is a sacrament of healing. At least one prayer to be said after receiving communion suggests that it is. In the name of Christ the priest prays that the body and blood of Christ may be 'a lasting remedy for *body and soul*'. Another prayer asks that we may be made one in Christ and since he is present in a unique way we may believe that he is present with all the love, compassion and power that he showed when he healed the sick during his earthly mission.

Christ continues his gesture of healing through the ministers of the sacrament but he is also in the sick and suffering in a special way. It is one of the oldest themes of the spiritual writers that the sick and suffering are made like Christ in his passion. But it is a matter of common experience that identification with the suffering of Christ is for most a matter of considerable difficulty. Illness and pain often seem like an unwarranted and undeserved assault on our personality and the reaction to them is often rebellion. To help us to overcome this Christ has given us the sacrament of his compassion, the sacrament of anointing, through which he offers to the sick his power to enable them to accept their condition and to unite their sufferings with his. Such acceptance often comes slowly and with difficulty but however weary we may be in mind and body, Christ is with us strengthening our faith and stimulating our love, and since through all the sacraments we share in his passion, death and resurrection in different ways, we can say that here we are made like him precisely in his suffering. We are conformed to Christ in his passion but that is not the end: as St Paul prayed that he might share his sufferings but only so that he might 'attain to the resurrection' (Philippians 3.10–11), so for the sick there remains the possibility of 'resurrection', restoration to health, or if death should supervene, resurrection with Christ. This is the hope that is held out to us and the sacrament of anointing strengthens that hope, a hope grounded in Christ who is with us and who will raise us up if it be his will.

THE PASSION

*

THERE is a tradition going back to the twelfth century, and perhaps a little before, of meditation on the physical sufferings of Jesus. There can be no doubt that it was fruitful in the lives of many saints and of other devout people. It has lasted until today and, as the devotion of the Stations of the Cross shows, it is still an important element in the prayer-life of many Christians. But it has two defects, the second more important than the first.

As one gets older meditation on the sufferings of Christ becomes more and more difficult. Feelings have to be 'pumped up' and one's reactions become anything but spontaneous. Perhaps too we have become more aware than people once were that prolonged meditation on physical suffering is not psychologically healthy. One manifestation of this was a sort of mystique of suffering that seems to have afflicted many devout people in the nineteenth century. To put the matter crudely, suffering is good for you, suffering is the lot of the Christian in this world and the Christian joy brought by the gospel seems to have been left out of account. The Good News was in danger of becoming the Bad News. Jesus did indeed suffer but his suffering was the way to joy, as the writer of the Letter to the Hebrews tells us: 'Let us look to Jesus, the pioneer and perfecter of our faith, who *for the joy that was set before him* endured the cross, despising the shame, and is seated at the right hand of God' (12.2).

The second defect of the tradition was that it lacked balance. In the later Middle Ages emphasis on the suffering Christ, depicted in the most horrific detail, became a distortion of the redeeming work of Christ. The saying of Jesus 'Was it not necessary that the Christ should suffer these things and enter into his glory?' seems to have been overlooked as were also the words of St Paul who wrote that Christ 'was put to death for our trespasses and raised for our justification' (Roman 4.25). The resurrection itself seems to have been regarded as an appendix, in the nineteenth century a topic for apologetics. According to the New Testament the crucifixion was the triumph over sin and death and evil and was the completion of the saving work and it was only because of the resurrection that the first Christians could see that the cross was a victory. Without the resurrection the cross was evidently a defeat and the disciples had to experience the resurrection before they could accept that it was in fact a victory and that 'joy had come into the world'.

Central to the ancient tradition of the first six centuries of the Church was the paschal mystery, the suffering, the death and the resurrection. This was and is the content of the great celebration that went on from Saturday evening to the morning of Easter Day. Lent was the preparation for it and Eastertime, the sacred Fifty Days, regarded as one day, was its continuation, the celebration of the Risen Lord who *through* suffering and death had brought salvation to those who had received him in faith. The restoration of the liturgy of Holy Week and Easter in our own time has done much to enable us to see once again that the paschal mystery is the dynamic centre of the Christian life. Through its celebration we are able to share in it, through it is communicated to us that which makes us Christians and enables us to go on living as children of God and brothers and sisters of Jesus Christ. Christ in his suffering, death and resurrection becomes the vital centre of our life, as he said in St John's gospel (7.28): 'He who believes in me, as the scripture has said, "Out of his heart shall flow rivers of living water".' The presence of the Risen Christ who suffered and died is real, his action within us is real, he with the Holy Spirit is the source of all we can think and do in relation to God. Indeed, since there is no separation of our human life from the Christ-life that is within us, that life can permeate *all* that we think or do or say. Christ with his Holy Spirit is the source of self-denial, of self-offering, of our prayer, he is the source of what is called mysticism. Every Christian who reflects on the divine presence is a potential mystic even if that potentiality is never realized in this life. To be 'in

Christ', in the Christ of the passion, death and resurrection, is to be united to him and through him to the Father by the working of the Holy Spirit.

The whole perspective of the paschal mystery and its celebration is very different from that of affective meditation on the physical sufferings of Christ which ran the risk of suggesting that Christ's sacrifice was something 'out there' and not something intimate to ourselves and our Christian living. For St Paul it was the very heart of the imitation of Christ, and the Christ he exhorted us to 'put on' was the Christ who had suffered and risen again so that we could live according to the fundamental pattern of *his* life, dying to self and rising with him by his power throughout all the ups and downs of our own life.

There was also the notion at one time that Christ's death was suffered 'for us' or 'instead of us', and while there is a truth in that it is not the whole truth. When at the Last Supper Jesus took some bread and broke it, and said 'This is my body which is being given up for you' he was giving *himself* not only for the disciples but *to* them, for 'body' meant his whole self. And when he said over the wine 'This is the blood of the covenant which is to be poured out for you and for many' he was offering his life to them, 'The life is in the blood'. What Jesus was forecasting then was that what he had to do could be done by no one but himself for sin had to be done away with 'for many', but also it was through the taking of the broken bread and the drinking of the wine that they were to be made one with him: 'He who eats my flesh and drinks my blood abides in me and I in him' (John 6.56). The cross and the supper are inseparable, they are two phases of the same redeeming action, and at the level of understanding it is almost certain that without the supper no one then or since would have seen the crucifixion as a sacrifice. The eucharist is the sacrament of the passion, death and resurrection that both shows the meaning of the cross and makes Christ present to us now.

But we have to try and penetrate more deeply the meaning of the words 'for us'. While it is true, as I have said, that Christ alone could do what was necessary to redeem us, he did not do it *apart* from us. He was one with us, he was one of us. By his taking of our human nature he became one of us, having the same nature which is ours, as we find in the ancient Christmas prayer in which we pray that we may be made partakers in his divine nature as he shared ours. St Paul underlined this when in his Letter to the Galatians (3.29) he said 'You are all one in Christ'. St Thomas Aquinas commenting on this said that the Head and members are, as it were, one mystical person (*quasi una mystica persona*), and he continues 'the satisfaction of Christ (brought about by the cross) belongs to all believers *as to his members*'. Further on he draws out the meaning of this statement: 'Christ's passion was the cause of the forgiveness of our sins by way of redemption. Because he is our Head, by his passion, which he bore out of love and obedience, he delivered us as his members from our sins.' Christ was the second Adam and like Adam he was the head of the human race, and, if the word be allowed, the organic head not a mere representative. He was so much one of us that what he did could be said to be done in us: 'It is as if a man redeemed himself from sin he had committed with his feet by means of a meritorious work he had performed with his hand.'[1] It follows that what Jesus did is ours but it has to be appropriated by faith, baptism and the eucharist, as St Paul makes clear: 'You are all sons of God through faith' and since the sons have been baptized into Christ they have put on Christ and it is the one bread that makes them all one body in Christ (1 Corinthians 10.17).

The paschal mystery then, in liturgical celebration, is the first and most important means whereby we become like Christ in his passion, death and resurrection. The content of the mystery has of course to be appropriated by each one of us and this we do in the first place by opening ourselves in faith and love to Christ who is offering himself to us in the whole range of the celebration. Given good will and generosity we can say that Christ is already at work within us, gradually changing our lowly bodies (our whole selves) until they begin to be like his glorious risen body (Philippians 3.21). No doubt it is the

[1] St Thomas Aquinas, *Summa Theologica,* III, 48, 2, ad 1; 49,I, ad 2.

process of a life-time and we have to be patient with ourselves but it should give us assurance and hope that Christ-likeness (the 'imitation of Christ') is gradually being formed within us.

That then is where it all begins, in the dynamism of the paschal mystery which is not simply a past event but a present reality. But, as suggested above, we have to live out the consequences of our membership with the paschal Christ day by day. Perhaps the first thing to be said is that that daily living is a sharing in the saving passion of Christ. And here St Leo has a word for us. Preaching during Lent, he recalled that it was a time of greater fasting 'so that by a common sharing (*commune consortium*) in the cross of Christ we might actively participate in what he did for us, according to the words of the Apostle "If we suffer with him, we shall also be glorified with him"' (Roman 8.17).[2] The context was the great fast but for Leo fasting was never separated from prayer and alms-giving. Prayer must support both and what was saved by fasting must be given to the needy. And although he mentions the Pauline text in connexion with fasting he goes on to speak of the daily life of the Christian. This has its tensions, its difficulties, its temptations and its anxieties and all these must be so handled that they may become means of sharing in the passion of Christ. The temptations must be resisted and the difficulties accepted and indeed the people must impose on themselves a certain discipline to prepare

[2] *De Quadragesima,* IX.

themselves for the infusion of new life that would be communicated to them by celebration of the paschal mystery. Meanwhile, in their struggles (and Leo uses the word *agonem*) Christ will be with them and they will be 'armed with the cross of Christ' (*Christi cruce armetur*). He will support them and strengthen them. To those who are actually suffering in one way or another he has another message, striking in its identification of such Christians with the suffering Christ: 'The sufferings of Christ are prolonged until the end of the world. . . *it is he who suffers in all who bear adversity* for righteousness' sake'.[3] It is significant of Leo's way of thinking that this statement comes in a sermon on the Passion.

Here I think we can find a whole programme of daily living. Even in the most mundane and necessary events of our life we can live in Christ and Christ is in our daily experience if we accept him into our lives. We need to 'see' him there and this will come through reflection and prayer. But it also shows that we have not to go off and do extraordinary things, there is no need to think that our hum-drum lives are less Christian than that of the enclosed monk or nun or than the heroic efforts of those who through the centuries the Church has called saints. Both can be an inspiration to us to live in Christ and both can help us with their prayers but unless we are called to such kinds of lives we can be on the way to union with God through Christ even as they are.

[3] *De Passione,* XIX.

THE RESURRECTION

*

AT least in Western Christianity it would seem that there has never been a worked-out spirituality of the resurrection. As we have seen, attention has been concentrated on the passion and death of Christ, sometimes and in some places to an extent that is disturbing. Perhaps this has had something to do with the psychology of the peoples of Western Europe, perhaps there was a deeper sense of sin. This seems to have been the case from about the ninth century onwards, as witness the private prayers marked by a deep sense of sin that were inserted into the Roman Mass for the personal use of the clergy. However that may be, the tradition of the Eastern churches seems to be rather different. Their liturgies reflect very consciously the heavenly liturgy and their very churches display the Lord of glory, the Pantocrator, before the eyes of the people; a Nicholas Cabasilas could write this of baptism:

> The resurrection, a free gift, is accorded to all ... who are willing to conform to the demands of this (new) life and of the Bridegroom, I mean to those who are born anew through the New Adam. They are resplendent with the radiance of grace that has penetrated them ...

> They hold their heads high like conquerors in the Olympic Games, because Christ is the crown. They listen because he is the Word. They lift up their eyes because he is the Sun and they are redolent of the fragrant perfume because he is Perfume (cf Song of Songs 1.3). Their garments are spotless on account of the wedding of the Bridegroom.[1]

Western readers may find the statement a bit high-pitched but that is how this fourteenth century Greek writer could think of the newly baptized. The Risen Lord is present throughout the liturgy, not least in baptism when people are made sons and daughters of God and members of the Risen Christ.

The paschal mystery and its celebration is once more clearly the centre of the liturgical year but it has yet to become the centre of the lives of most of us. Psychologically it is easier to identify with the Passion since suffering of one kind or another is the lot of everyone, even if we make a rather poor hand at accepting it. We are aware of our weakness of purpose and that we are weighed down by what St Paul called the body of sin. There is so much in us that is unregenerate, as yet unaffected by the redeeming power of Christ. Nonetheless it would be a start if we reflected that we are brothers and sisters of the *Risen* Christ and that his power is at work in us 'changing our lowly body to be like his glorious body' (Philippians 3.21). If this is to happen we need to

[1] *La Vie en Jésus-Christ,* p. 65.

open ourselves to his action, to be submissive to his will and, as far as in us lies, to collaborate with the divine work: 'God is at work in you, both to will and to work' according to his will (Philippians 2.11).

How then can we endeavour to live the resurrection? We can do so first by faith. From the New Testament onwards Christ's resurrection has been seen as the guarantee of the authenticity of our faith in Jesus, Son of God and the son of man, risen from the dead, and of all that he said and did. This was the faith of the apostles, summed up in the well known phrase of St Paul 'If Christ has not been raised, then our preaching is vain and your faith is vain' (1 Corinthians 15.14). The apostles and many others ('more than five hundred') were witnesses to the reality of the resurrection, and that Christ rose from the dead is in the strictest sense the apostolic faith of the Church. But, as we know, in more recent times the resurrection has become a matter of contention rather than a support of faith. This is not the place to pursue it but perhaps it may be said, without oversimplifying a complex problem, that the *language* to be used of the resurrection is one of the great difficulties. Does 'spiritual' mean unreal? St Paul did not seem to think so 'It is sown a physical body, it is raised a spirtual body' (1 Corinthians 15.44) and the 'body' he is talking about is the body of a human being who will be raised from the dead in the general resurrection. As with the human being there is identity between the 'physical' and the 'spiritual', for otherwise the whole process of resurrection would be meaningless, so with Christ. As a modern theologian has observed very reasonably:

> The empty tomb very powerfully expresses the *personal continuity* between the earthly Jesus and the risen Christ. Alongside or even despite all the transformation of a resurrection which make the risen Christ the anticipated beginning of the end of the world, he remains personally identical with the Jesus who lived and died. He does not appear as some kind of replica in his place. There is genuine identity in transformation.[2]

Perhaps the doubters and those who agonize over the resurrection forget that it is a mystery, a mystery of faith, which, like all the others, we accept on the testimony of the apostles and the early Christians who *saw* the Lord, but also like those mysteries it can never be totally comprehended. Difficulties remain and will always remain but if Christ did not rise we should be of all people the most miserable and our faith would be vain, empty, and the preaching of the apostles and the existence of the Church would be without explanation. In humble and enquiring faith, a faith that is always seeking to understand (*fides quaerens intellectum*), we accept the resurrection with joy, a joy the Church has expressed throughout the centuries with its many Alleluias. That is the first characteristic in fact of the Christian who believes in the resurrection of Christ.

[2] Gerald O'Collins, *Interpreting Jesus* (1983), pp. 128–129.

In the circumstances in which we live with all the pressures and difficulties of modern life it will not be easy to sustain a sentiment of joy. But a security of faith, which must not be allowed to relapse into self-satisfaction, is some guarantee that we shall be able to do so. We have heard the Good News, we have seen the whole life of Christ displayed before us, we have been made one with the Christ who suffered, died and rose again for us and this should give us assurance and a quiet joy. If it seems difficult to express this, we may reflect that what we are in the depths of our being expresses itself in ways of which we are quite unconscious. The Christian who goes about his or her work, who cares for others and who, if the occasion arises, can speak of the faith that is in them without aggression or self-righteousness, will be conveying something of the joy that is in his or her heart.

Most of us have met at one time or another people whom we naturally think of as holy, perhaps an old monk or nun, who, though they have much physical suffering to bear, yet have a serenity or tranquillity of spirit. Almost certainly without knowing it something of the joy of the resurrection has penetrated their lives and they are living by it. That comes very like to a saying of St Thomas: we are living in the third era, the era of the resurrection, and the eternal life is already beginning in us.[3] This too seems to be an echo of St John 'if anyone eats of this bread he will

[3] S.T. III, 53.

live for ever; and the bread which I shall give for *the life of the world* is my flesh' (6.51). In the eucharist we are in communion with the Risen Christ and the life he offers us is the eternal life which begins in us now. The seed of eternal life is implanted in us in baptism when we are made like Christ not only in his suffering and death but also in his resurrection (Romans 6.5) and the seed is destined to grow into the light of glory through our participation in him in the eucharist. The process may be long and arduous, rendered imperfect by our weakness and falls, but, as long as we remain faithful, the beginnings of eternal life will be brought to fruition.

Perhaps too we need to remember that it is the Risen Christ who is the source of life. He is the life, as well as the way and the truth, he is the vine of which believing and baptized Christians are the branches, he with the Holy Spirit is the giver of life: 'He who drinks of the water that I shall give him will never thirst; the water that I shall give him will become in him a spring of water welling up to eternal life', and 'If anyone thirst, let him come to me and drink. He who believes in me, as the scripture has said, "Out of his heart shall flow rivers of living water". Now this he said about the Spirit which those who believed were to receive; for as yet the Spirit had not been given, because Jesus was not yet glorified' (John 4.14; 7.37–39).

There may be a question as to what this life is. It is *like* water, it is *like* the sap rising from the trunk into the branches but it is communicated by the Holy Spirit who is like fire (Acts 2) and fire is powerful, fire has a dreadful energy. We can pursue this image in a very different place. In a sentence in Ephesians 1.19 we find 'energy' (*energeian*), 'power' (*kratous*) and strength (*ischuos*) that the Father gives to those who 'know' Christ: 'what are the riches of his glorious inheritance in the saints, and what is the immeasurable greatness of his power *in us* who believe, according to the working of his *great might* which he accomplished in Christ when he raised him from the dead.' It seems fair to say that the 'life' is something working (energizing) in those who accept the Risen Christ by faith. This is the work of the Holy Spirit of the Risen Christ, as the text makes clear later on: (I pray) 'that according to the riches of his glory he may grant you to be strengthened (empowered) with might through the Spirit in the inner man, and that Christ may dwell in your hearts' (3.16–17). These are very vigorous expressions and they indicate that the power of the Risen Christ is within us so that we can live 'the new kind of life' that he communicates to us by the Holy Spirit.

This is what we *are* and it may be helpful to realize something of 'the riches of the glory' that are within us; it would be a good thing when we 'set our minds on things that are above' (Colossians 3.2) if we remembered that these things are already within us, as St Paul himself indeed suggests for when following up that injunction he adds 'For you have died and your life is hidden with Christ in God' (Colossians 3.3). As he said in another place and in a very different context, God is not far from us and 'in him we live and move and have our being' (Acts 17.27–28). But it is not an abstract deity who is with us but the incarnate Son of God who rose again, not to leave us but to be closer to us than he was even to his disciples, through the Holy Spirit who makes him present to us in a new and more intimate way.

It may be granted that it is difficult to live the resurrection or rather to live out the risen life to which we are committed by baptism but it is no more difficult than to live the sharing in the passion of Christ to which we are also called. But if we reflect that the very purpose of the resurrection was that Christ might be with us, that he might be in the world, invisibly but really, we might gradually come to have a sense that the power of Christ is not only with us but that he is with others and is present in a world that seems to be totally devoid of him. By his self-humiliation and resurrection he is Lord, Lord of the world, and its destiny is in his hands. As will be remembered, the Book of the Apocalypse describes him as 'Lord of lords and King of kings' and, however obscure that book may be in many places, it was intended as a message of comfort to Christians who were confronted with a mighty and totally pagan empire.

All this is but to say that one message of the resurrection is hope, hope not only that we shall rise again but hope that is grounded on a present reality, namely the 'energizing' of the Risen Christ within us who has already intiated the process whereby we can enter into the glory of the children of God.

Hope, then, and faith and a joy engendered by faith, and life flowing from the Risen Christ, these would seem to be the elements of a spirituality of the resurrection.

THE ASCENSION

*

THE Ascension is in some ways more difficult to grasp than the resurrection. According to the Acts of the Apostles it took place forty days after the resurrection. In Matthew we find the apostles in Galilee almost immediately after the resurrection, and the ascension is not mentioned at all. In the famous appendix to Mark, Jesus appears to the apostles 'as they sat at table', apparently on Easter Day itself, and immediately the 'Lord Jesus, after he had spoken to them, was taken up into heaven, and sat down at the right hand of God' (16.14–19). In Luke the order of events is the same. After the meal Jesus led them out as far as Bethany, 'and lifting up his hands he blessed them. While he blessed them, he parted from them, and was carried up to heaven' (24.50–51). In the gospel according to St John there is no *description* at all. Only in Acts do we find a description. What are we to make of it all? The first reflexion that occurs is that the pictorial description of Acts is not of primary importance. What the evangelists and St Paul emphasize in their different ways is the *meaning* of the event. For Matthew, for Luke (gospel and Acts) the event marks the beginning of *mission:* 'Go and make disciples of all nations . . . ' and 'you shall be my witnesses . . . to the end of the earth.' But in the Marcan appendix there is a little phrase that seems to echo St Paul: 'and (he) sat down at the right hand of God'. Paul writes in Colossians: 'If then you have been raised with Christ, seek the things that are above, *where Christ is seated at the right hand of God*' (3.1–2 and compare Ephesians 2.5).

The deeper meaning of the ascension, then, seems to be that it is the *exaltation* of Christ when he achieves the Lordship of the world for which 'seated at the right hand of God' is the metaphor. This is a theme that is elaborated in the Letter to the Ephesians: 'Therefore it is said, "When he ascended on high he led a host of captives, and he gave gifts to men" . . . He who descended is he who ascended far above all the heavens that he might fill all things' (4.8–10). This represents his victory over the mysterious 'principalities and powers, the rulers of this present darkness and the spiritual hosts of wickedness in the heavenly places' (6.12 and cf Colossians 1.16). He is Lord of all, Lord of everything in heaven and on earth, and his ascension marks his accession to that lordship. But that does not mean he will abandon the disciples and leave them orphans; he will come back to them (John 14.18) and he will be with them 'manifesting' himself to them. As well as that, his ascension will give the impetus to mission (and so we rejoin Matthew and Luke) and marks the time of the outpouring of gifts for that mission and the building up of the Church: 'And his gifts were that some should be apostles, some prophets, some evangelists, some pastors and teachers, to equip the saints for the work of ministry, for the building up of the body of Christ' (Ephesians 4.11–12).

St Paul, then, chose to put the ascension in the context of 'the body of Christ' in which we are to 'grow up into him who is the head' (4.15). St Leo, following St Augustine, develops this thought in his two sermons on the ascension. It is *our* human nature, he emphasizes, that is raised up above angels and archangels until that same nature (in him) takes its place with the Father and, united to the Son, shares in the glory of the Father. That is why Leo could say that Christ's ascension is *our* exaltation of advancement (*provectio*) too. His insight into the meaning of the ascension is penetrating. Not content with what he has already said, he goes on to say that in hope the body is with the glorified Head and that in hope we have penetrated with him to the heights of heaven. He who has made us his members has placed us at the right hand of the Father, and we enter into the new Paradise of which the old was but a symbol. That, says Leo, is why the apostles rejoiced.[1]

The foregoing is the meaning, perhaps the princi-

[1] The phrase *Christi ascensio est nostra provectio* has been inserted into the opening prayer of the feast but is not well translated (cf also Preface I).

pal meaning, of the ascension. It is not an event that concerns Christ alone but, like all the other great events of his life, it was *for* us, not simply as a moral exhortation 'to seek those things that are above' but as an anticipation of what we shall be, of what we are becoming if we try and live 'in Christ'. In the 'spiritual' life there is a certain dynamic and the *dynamis*, the dynamic power, is in Jesus Christ, and it is he who draws us: 'No one comes to the Father except by me' (John 14.6) and the impetus is given by the Holy Spirit.

The mention of the Spirit brings us to an even deeper insight into the meaning of the ascension. In chapter 7.39 John says that the Spirit had not yet been given because Jesus was not yet 'glorified' and in chapter 20 we find him giving the Spirit: 'He breathed on them and said to them "Receive the Holy Spirit. If you forgive the sins of any, they are forgiven; if you retain the sins of any, they are retained".' And this in turn is but to fulfil that mysterious 'giving (up) of the Spirit' that John describes as the last act of Jesus: 'He bowed his head and gave up his spirit' which the Latin translates very well, '*tradidit spiritum*', he gave over or handed on the spirit. From an early age in the Church the 'spirit' has been thought to have been the 'Holy Spirit'. It is the Risen Christ who gives the Spirit, it is the Risen Christ who is the source of the Spirit who infuses the divine life that 'flows like living waters' within us

(John 7.38).[2] The first instance of this is the giving of the Spirit to the apostles and here we see the close connection in John between the resurrection (and even the death), the ascension and the sending or giving of the Holy Spirit at Pentecost. John's vision of things transcends time and space, he is concerned with the inner reality of the culmination of the saving 'work' that Jesus came into the world to do. Not that he denies the reality of the events he records in his gospel or the events described by Luke in Acts but always he is seeking their inner meaning. It is also an illustration of the closeness to each other in the liturgy of Christ's death, resurrection, and ascension and the sending of the Spirit. The vision of the liturgy is very Johannine; the paschal mystery issues into the giving of the Spirit and it is significant that the feasts of the ascension and Pentecost, as they are usually understood, came into the liturgical year only in the late fourth century long after the sacred Fifty Days had been established.

There remain all those sayings of Jesus in the Last Supper discourses of St John's Gospel. Jesus will go away but in a little time he will come back again, the disciples will at first be sad but will then rejoice. In one sense he will be absent from them, in another he will be with them and indeed living in them. These

[2] The 'his' in the passage is a little ambiguous. Some commentators think that it means the heart of Jesus. Even so, it is his life that flows into us by the operation of the Holy Spirit.

sayings and many more are mysterious and difficult to understand. Do the 'little time' sayings refer to the time after the resurrection or do they look beyond it? Probably to both though the weight of learned opinion is that they refer to the time between the resurrection and the ascension. However, it is characteristic of the author of the Fourth Gospel to have two time-scales in mind. The 'glory' of the cross is the glory of the resurrection, reflected back on the cross. The 'little time' is the time of the appearances but it points on to the age of the Spirit when the disciples and their followers will bear witness to Christ and will suffer for doing so. This 'time' or day in turn reaches on to the final judgement 'when those in their tombs will come forth' (5.29) and there will be the final separation of the good from the bad. The whole era from the resurrection to the End, the *eschaton*, is a between-time when always there is the tension between the 'then' and the 'now'. Christ has come, Christ will come again but there is always the 'now' and the mysterious words in these discourses seem to be telling us something about the 'now', that is the post-resurrection and the post-ascension time in which we have to live. Is Christ present or absent? 'I will not abandon you, I will not leave you orphans.' But how is he present? Is he present more than by hope? 'I will come again and take you to myself.' He is present by love; 'If you love me you will keep my commandments.' He is present because he dwells in us: 'If a man loves me, he will keep my word, and my

Father will love him, and he will come to him and make our home with him.' But that presence, that indwelling, is effected by the Holy Spirit: 'I will ask the Father and he will give you another Counsellor to be with you for ever, even the Spirit of truth' who dwells with you and will be with you (14.3,21,23,16,17).

The presence is a *real* presence. It is perceived by faith, it is aspired to by hope but it is real and immediate because the Spirit makes it so. The whole Christ, not just some sort of ghost, is present to us, the Christ of glory who left his disciples, who left Mary Magdalen, who left his Mother, so that through the Holy Spirit he might be really present to them and to all believing Christians to the end of time. It was only in this way that he *could* be present to us and as far as we can penetrate the mystery of the risen and ascended Christ—and perhaps we ought to remember that it *is* a mystery—this is why we ascended to his Father. His physical presence had to be transcended; 'Mary, do not cling to me', do not cling to me in my 'natural' appearance; I must go to my Father *so that* I can be closer to you, more intimate to you—*intimior intimo tuo*, in the words of St Augustine— than I ever have been on earth.

St Augustine saw something of this when, putting the event in the context of the Church as the body of Christ, he said, 'Christ, while in heaven, is also with us; and we, while on earth, are also with him. He is with us in his godhead and his power and his love;

and we, though we cannot be with him in godhead as he is with us, can be with him in our love, our love for him.' And this 'because of the unity between us and himself, for he is our head and we are his body'. What Augustine wants to say is that presence means action; there is a kind of interaction by faith and love, a sort of *living with* Christ who through his Holy Spirit stimulates faith—'the Holy Spirit, whom the Father will send in my name, will teach you all things'—and prompts our love so that we may respond to Christ and go out of ourselves to him. Living is loving and loving is living and that is how Christ is present to us—by the Holy Spirit. To repeat, the Holy Spirit makes possible the presence of the risen, ascended Christ to us now.[3]

St Leo, as we have seen, also puts the ascension in the context of the mystical body, he too emphasizes the importance of faith and love but he has a pregnant phrase which brings us to the liturgy itself: 'What our Redeemer did visibly has passed over into the sacraments.'[4] *Quod Redemptoris nostri conspicuum fuit,* all that could be seen, all that he did, is now invisibly present in the liturgy. The *opus redemptionis*, the work of our salvation, has in some way 'passed over' into the sacraments where Christ is active and available to us. In a sense too, Christ is 'visible' to us and many

[3] Translation and quotations from Second Reading for the Ascension as in *The Divine Office,* II, p. 627.

[4] *De Ascensione,* II.

writers on the liturgy have said that Christ is 'manifested' in and through it, as indeed the Constitution on the Liturgy (41) says of the communal celebrations of that same liturgy. It is the 'epiphany' of the active presence of Christ by the Holy Spirit who is operative over its whole range (see the two epicleses of the eucharistic prayers). The liturgy is the 'place' of the presence of Christ but as in his life-time he required a faith aspiring to love in those who approached him, so he requires it of us now. The liturgy is not just a series of services 'out there' in which we take part by speaking and singing.

Christ is present and active but his presence and action can only be realized in us if we are present to him by faith and love. True, both are strengthened and activated by him but he can only reach us, so to say, if we go to him in that spirit. As we read in St John, God requires that we should be worshippers in spirit and in truth (John 4.23) and if they are right who would spell 'spirit' with a capital 'S', then we can see that it is the Spirit in us who makes possible such worship.

One result of our reflections is that in the death, the resurrection and ascension of Christ the Holy Spirit is active throughout, and no doubt that is why St Paul so often calls the Spirit the Spirit of the Lord, the Spirit of Christ. If the reality has to be spelt out in events so that we can even begin to understand it, the great work of redemption is really one thing, one divine act, effected by Jesus in the power of the Holy

Spirit, and through the Spirit the Risen and ascended Christ is present to his people now as he will be throughout the ages. And what was affected so long ago is actualized in all those who celebrate the mysteries (*sacramenta*) in the Spirit,[5] with faith and love.

[5] What I have been trying to say is that the Risen and ascended Christ is present to us and though it may be described as a 'spiritual' presence it is nonetheless real. Christ ascended from this earth so that he might be *nearer* to us than if he had remained. It is in his glorified body, totally filled with the Spirit, that he is with us and the nearness is possible only to the glorified Christ. But the presence with us of the Holy Spirit is also indispensable. I find that some confirmation of this is given by the distinguished exegete Raymond E. Brown: 'Until Jesus returns to take them with him to his heavenly dwelling place (xiv.2–3, xvii.24), believers shall not see him physically but only in and through the Holy Spirit' (*The Gospel according to John*, II, p. 713). And again: 'The later Christian is no further removed from the ministry of Jesus than was the earlier Christian.' Hence, 'Blessed are those who have not seen yet believe.'

PENTECOST

*

'PENTECOST' means the fiftieth day, the fiftieth day from Easter Sunday. It marked the end of the Fifty Days of Paschal or Eastertide which were regarded as the continuation of the one Great Sunday when the Church was renewed by the celebration of the Paschal Mystery. This is why by the third century, at least in Rome and in some though not in all other places, the sacraments of initiation, baptism, confirmation and the eucharist could also be celebrated on the Fiftieth Day. As at Easter there was a Vigil which lasted from the evening of Saturday until Sunday morning. Until the late fourth century the Ascension event was also celebrated in the liturgy of this day—greatly to the confusion of the modern mind, though it was based on the vision of St Luke's gospel and on that of St John which in this matter were not based on linear time. As we have seen, the 'glory' of the Johannine gospel included the cross, the resurrection and the ascension. You could say that St John read history backwards; he saw the cross through the resurrection and the ascension or, if you like, from the viewpoint of the exaltation of the Risen Christ. It meant that the liturgy of Pentecost was very rich in content. Thus, for instance, Christians saw the Christ completing his work of salvation, he himself being the first of those who rise again, and carrying the 'first-fruits' of salvation to the Father. He led captivity captive but also 'gave gifts to men' (Ephesians 4.8), and first of all the great gift, the Holy Spirit, which he so to say released into the Church.

The early Church was also conscious of the many parallels with the Old Testament. Pentecost with its many languages spoken by the apostles was the counterpart of the making of the Tower of Babel with its many languages the sign of the division of the human race. Now the gift of the Holy Spirit becomes the unifying force of redeemed humanity: 'they were all of one mind and heart'. The Law was given on Sinai by Moses and the new 'Law' was announced by the Holy Spirit who dwells in the heart of the new Israel and in the heart of every Christian. Some of those elements can still be discerned in the liturgy of Pentecost[1] but the separation of the Ascension from it lessened its content, especially the offering of the first-fruits of redeemed humanity.

The development of the feast of the ascension came slowly. It is first attested only in the last two decades of the fourth century in both East and West and marks the first breach in the sacred Fifty Days.

[1] See the Vigil Mass, the opening prayer; the first reading, Genesis 11, the Tower of Babel; the second, the giving of the Law, Exodus 19.

Gradually Pentecost too became a separate feast, almost wholly concerned with the sending of the Holy Spirit. The cessation of Pentecost as the second great occasion of Christian initiation, at least in the West, further loosened the connection with Easter, though where the catechumenate has been restored the link is once more apparent.

However an attentive reading of the liturgical texts of both the Vigil and the Feast shows that the relation between Easter and Pentecost has been kept. The opening prayer of the Vigil speaks of the *paschale sacramentum* which has been celebrated throughout the Fifty Days and prays that people of all races and languages may be gathered into one by the gift, which must mean the gift of the Spirit. The third reading (Ezekiel 37.1–14) and the fourth (Joel 3.1–5) tell of the outpouring of the Spirit on the old Israel for its renewal. But the most interesting is the brief gospel, John 7.37–39: 'If any man is thirsty, let him come to me! Let the man come and drink who believes in me! As the scripture says: From his breast shall flow fountains of living water. *He was speaking of the Spirit which those who believed in him were to receive; for there was no Spirit as yet because Jesus had not yet been glorified.*' As we have seen, the glorification of Jesus was in the Johannine mind inseparable from the cross, the resurrection and the ascension. The sending of the Spirit was the work of the Risen Lord as is made amply clear by the gospel passage of the Mass of the Feast: 'Receive the Holy Spirit ...' (John 20.22) which is a repetition of the gospel for the Second Sunday in Easter time. Here the Lord on the very day he rose from the dead gives the Holy Spirit to the apostles. It is, as it were, the first-fruits of his resurrection.

As a liturgical scholar has written: 'The gift of the Spirit is inseparable from the exaltation of the Lord as together they constitute the completion of the work of redemption and the inauguration of the new era that prepares the way for the Parousia.'[2] It is a vision that may trouble modern minds conditioned by clock-time but it is the vision of St John's gospel and largely of the liturgy itself. Even in the current liturgy the connection between the 'glorification' of Christ and the giving of the Spirit are put beyond doubt by the choice of the gospel readings for Year B (John 15.26–27; 16.12–15) and Year C (John 14.15–16, 23–26). This last, '(The Father) will give you another Counsellor ... The Counsellor the Holy Spirit, whom the Father will send in my name, he will teach you all things ...' is found in the oldest stratum of the ancient feast when glorification and the giving of the Spirit were celebrated in one feast.

Once, however, Pentecost had become a separate feast the link between the Fifty Days was seriously weakened. It has become the Feast of the Holy Spirit in popular estimation though, even as the liturgy of the day is now, the link can be discerned. In the first

[2] R. Cabié, *La Pentecôte* (1965), p. 83.

part of the eucharistic prayer (the 'Preface') we give thanks to the Father through the Son for the sending of the Holy Spirit so bringing the paschal mystery to its culmination (*sacramentum paschale consummans*). And in the prayer over the offerings the coming of the Spirit promised by the Son prays that thereby the mystery of the sacrifice may be revealed to us, the self-offering of Christ that is at the very heart of the paschal mystery. If we add to these texts the gospel of Year C we find that Pentecost in the Roman rite does not concentrate exclusively on the Holy Spirit. There we read 'I shall ask the *Father* and he will give you another Advocate (Counsellor) to be with you for ever' and with him will be the Father and the Son who will make their home with those who love God. As in the Byzantine rite where this Sunday is called Pentecost: the Feast of the Holy Trinity, so with ours we have a suggestion that might fruitfully be taken up.

As in the earliest days Pentecost was seen as a feast of the first-fruits, we have here a comparable notion of fruition. The work of redemption beginning with the birth of Jesus and continuing in the passion, death, resurrection and ascension comes to completion. The mystery of redemption is the work of Father, Son and Holy Spirit and we are reminded of the basic rhythm of the liturgy which is directed *to* the Father *through* the Son *in* the Holy Spirit, and if that is true of the Mass it is also true of the whole Liturgical Year. And this is a kind of 'sacrament' of the deep mystery of God himself, the mutual indwelling of the Three Persons in one another, an indwelling that we can 'understand' as the ceaseless self-giving of the Three Persons in love, a love that is never exhausted. From out of the heart of that self-giving comes forth the Word who, in the phrase of St Thomas Aquinas, is *Verbum spirans Amorem,*[3] the Word breathing out the Holy Spirit who is Love personified. From him the love that is God flows out on all those redeemed by Jesus Christ so that they are being carried back into the intimate life of the Godhead: 'he who loves me will be loved by my Father and I will love him and manifest myself to him . . . and we will come to him and make our home with him.' Living in Christ means living in the depths of the life and love of God.

In this sense the culmination or 'completion' of the work of salvation, as the translation of the Missal calls it, must go on to the end of time and to the end of the life of each one of us. This work of salvation continues in the Church, for the whole Church is the charismatic body of Christ, indwelt by the Holy Spirit who with us prays ceaselessly to the Lord 'Come' (Apocalypse 22.17) and each member of the body can and should cry out 'Come, Lord Jesus, come'. Living thus in the Spirit, the whole body is built up until 'we become the perfect Man, fully mature with the fulness of Christ' (Ephesians 4.13) in whom dwells

[3] *Summa Theologica*, I, q.43, a5, ad 2um.

'the fulness of the Godhead' (Colossians 2.9). The Church, that is the whole people of God, breathes and lives and moves in the Holy Spirit who was given to it on the cross (John 19.30), after the resurrection, and publicly for all to see on the great day of Pentecost.

That giving of the Spirit continues in baptism, in confirmation, in penance, in ordination, in the eucharist when the worshipping community invoke him on themselves, and in the annual celebration of Pentecost. The Word breathes into us the Love that is the Spirit so that, as we pray in the *Veni Sancte Spiritus,* he may totally permeate our being. He comes to fill our minds ('Holy Spirit, Lord of Light') so that our faith may be deepened until it becomes a kind of knowledge, *gnosis*, which in turn is destined to grow into the light of glory when we shall see God 'as he is'. He comes to take possession of hearts, 'Bend the stubborn heart and will', so that we may give ourselves to him. With the very love that he 'kindles' in our hearts we can respond to him, we can go out from our ego and begin or continue our return to God.

But since our rooted selfishness is the one obstacle that can block the action of the Holy Spirit in mind and heart we pray that he will 'our inmost being fill' and 'Heal our wounds, our strength renew, on our dryness pour thy dew, wash the stains of guilt away.'

If then we let God have his way with us we can enter into his life through the Son and by the power of the Holy Spirit. We can become sharers in that love that is breathed out between them. We can begin to think the thoughts of God or, if that seems too bold a statement, we can begin to see this world and ourselves and all our involvement in the world from God's viewpoint. This, said St Thomas, is Wisdom,[4] the highest of the seven gifts (the *sacrum septenarium* —the sevenfold gifts) for which we pray on the feast of Pentecost. We can begin to desire what God wants of us and this is to do his will wherein is our peace: *In la sua voluntate è nostra pace* (in his will is our peace). We can breathe with the very breath of God—in the Holy Spirit. This is what we are destined for, this is the goal of all prayer and the purpose of the whole Christian life until all is consummated in the vision of God.

The Holy Spirit is at work in the Church, in ourselves and, says the liturgy somewhat surprisingly, in the physical world: 'Send forth your Spirit, and they shall be created and you will renew the face of the earth.' Whether you accept the future tense or, as correctly in all modern translations, the present tense, it is a puzzling statement. In the psalm (103 (104)) the verse refers primarily to the animal creation which, however, is seen in the framework of the physical universe. One wonders how the Holy Spirit can operate in either. However, the psalm is a poetic re-writing of Genesis 1 and the spirit of God (*pneuma Theou*, in the Greek)[5] is seen as the creative divine

[4] S.T. II, ii, q.45, a.1. [5] As in Wisdom 1.7.

force that brought the physical universe into existence but this is not static, it is in a continuous process of becoming. It is by the 'breath of God' that the material world is sustained now and without it it would disintegrate and return to its primeval chaos: 'You hide your face, they are dismayed; you take back your spirit, they die, returning to the dust from which they came.' For the writers of the Old Testament the world was an unfinished universe moving towards a consummation the nature of which could be hardly glimpsed. It was a vision of things found also in St Paul: 'The creation waits with *eager longing* (as if animated) for the revealing of the sons of God . . . the creation itself will be set free from its bondage to decay and obtain the glorious liberty of the children of God' (Romans 8.19,21). Until recently we have forgotten that the physical world, the vegetable world and the animal world interpenetrate each other and, as we are coming to realize ever more vividly, are dependent on each other. If this realization is ever lost and if we treat the universe as something to be endlessly exploited it will be destroyed and the human race with it.

This 'animation' of the universe cannot be stated in philosophical concepts or in the terms of the physical sciences and since C. H. Dodd in his commentary on the Epistle to the Romans (p. 134) calls St Paul's view a 'truly poetical conception', we may have recourse to a poet for enlightenment:

. . . . . .
The world is charged with the grandeur of God.
It will flame out, like shining from shook foil;
And for all this, nature is never spent;
There lives the dearest freshness deep down things;
And though the last lights off the back black West went
Oh, the morning, at the brown brink eastward, springs—
Because the Holy Ghost over the bent
World broods with warm breast and with ah! bright wings.[6]

If the Holy Spirit is present in the cosmos he is present as a unifying force, he is seen in the liturgy of Pentecost as the principle of unity in the human being and in the Church. The whole personality is integrated or perhaps we ought to say re-integrated: 'Our bodies through the water of baptism have received the unity which leads to freedom from corruption; but our souls have received it through the Holy Spirit' (Irenaeus, 2nd Reading of the Office). But unity is an inadequate word here; it seems to signify a unity already achieved and complete. What the liturgy is saying is that the Holy Spirit is *dynamis*, the dynamic force, unifying the Church, the human race, each individual and the whole cosmos. As we pray in the opening prayer of the Vigil of Pentecost: 'By your grace gather together the scattered and divided nations and make them one body to the glory

[6] Gerard Manley Hopkins, 'God's Grandeur'.

of your name.' As the Holy Spirit is the dynamic power making the Risen Christ present to us now, so he will be at the end of time when the Church will become *in fact* the 'sacrament' of the whole human race, lifted up in praise and thanksgiving, finally the 'perfect gift' offered to the Father by Christ the Lord in the power of the Holy Spirit.